Children with Cerebral Palsy

KT-162-222

WITHDRAWN

NAPIER UNIVERSITY LIS

Children with Cerebral Palsy

A Manual for Therapists, Parents and Community Workers

Archie Hinchcliffe

Illustrations by Barbara Lynne Price

ITDG PUBLISHING

COM
618.9283606HIN

First published by Vistaar Publications,
a division of Sage Publications India Pvt Ltd,
in collaboration with

ITDG Publishing
103–105 Southampton Row, London WC1B 4HL, UK
www.itdgpublishing.org.uk

© Archie Hinchcliffe 2003

First published in 2003
Reprinted with corrections in 2003

ISBN 1 85339 565 X

All rights reserved. No part of this publication may be reprinted or reproduced or utilised in any form
or by any electronic, mechanical, or other means, now known or hereafter invented, including
photocopying and recording, or in any information storage or retrieval system, without the written
permission of the publishers.

For copyright reasons, this edition is not for sale in India, Pakistan, Bangladesh,
Sri Lanka, Nepal, Bhutan and the Maldives.

A catalogue record for this book is available from the British Library.

ITDG Publishing is the publishing arm of the Intermediate Technology Development Group.
Our mission is to build the skills and capacity of people in developing countries through the
dissemination of information in all forms, enabling them to improve the quality of their lives
and that of future generations.

Typeset by Star Compugraphics, New Delhi
Printed by Antony Rowe Ltd, Wiltshire

To those children with
cerebral palsy and their families, and to the therapists and
community workers that I have been privileged to know.

Contents

Acknowledgements

This book was written for the many physiotherapists who attended the courses I taught in different countries in Africa and the Middle East. I am indebted to them for the encouragement they have given me to write and the friendship they showed to me during the courses.

In order to teach it is necessary to reflect to one's own learning, and my reflection causes me to be deeply grateful for the opportunities I have had to attend Bobath courses and study days. From these I learnt not only about cerebral palsy and the way it affects a child but also a problem solving way of thinking. The tutors on these courses were invaluable inspirational role models.

I am also greatly indebted to the many wise and experienced mentors who guided me in the writing and the putting together of the book, chief among these is David Werner who wrote *Disabled Village Children*. He took hours of painstaking trouble to check the drawings and provide thoughtful and apt advice on sections of the text. He was kind enough to say that he learnt a lot about cerebral palsy through reading the book.

During my many years of working with children with cerebral palsy, I have been blessed by coming in contact with people who have helped me to see the children more holistically and less as patients. Chris Underhill, who established Action on Disability and Development (ADD), and his Ugandan counterpart, Charles Langwa-Ntale, gave me the opportunity to understand how to link rehabilitation into the process of development as a whole. Peter Coleridge, who wrote *Disability, Liberation and Development* and who invited me to teach a course in Afghanistan, has also been a good friend and source of inspiration.

The book would not have been complete without the contributions of Marian Browne and Jean Westmacott. I am deeply grateful for the efforts they put in to write about eating and drinking and about the wonderfully useful APT (Appropriate Paper-based Technology). I also want to thank Lynne Price for all her gifted work on the drawings.

But without the help and support of my husband, Peter, this book would certainly never have been written. In all our postings abroad, he made sure that my work with children took precedence over my duties as a diplomatic wife and he has constantly encouraged me in the writing of this book.

Finally, I want to thank my daughter, Clare, who took great trouble to sort out a tangle I had made in Chapters 2 and 3. With clinical incisiveness, she took the strands of the tangle apart and the words fell into clear understandable sentences. What a gift!

Introduction

This book has been written with therapists in mind. It is for therapists with whom I worked, and who attended courses that I conducted in the Middle East, Afghanistan and Africa. But I hope that community workers, volunteers, teachers, programme managers and parents too will find ideas and information in the book that will help them understand the nature of cerebral palsy and how to help children affected by it.

During the eighties and nineties I lived in the Middle East and Africa, huge changes took place in attitudes to the provision of services to children with disabilities. In the seventies, funding agencies were supporting hospital-based programmes and institutional care. Considerable amounts of aid money were spent on training physiotherapists (never occupational therapists or speech and language therapists). But this approach to rehabilitation (the medical model) was seen to fail when it was realised how very few children could benefit from it. Even those few children who learnt to walk with aids and who received education during their time in the institutions, could not be easily re-integrated into their communities.

This failure, and a powerful move by organisations of disabled people, led to the development of the social model, and the switch of donor funding to community-based rehabilitation (CBR) programmes.

There is no doubt that CBR and the philosophy behind it has achieved huge benefits for disabled children and their families. The programmes, when they work well, mobilise the whole community so that the child and his or her family become accepted and supported by it. Ownership and responsibility for the success of the programme is with the people on the ground. This was a very attractive idea for donors, many of whom unfortunately thought that this would be a cheap way of dealing with a problem that otherwise seemed like a bottomless pit. This short-term view did not take into account the fact that it is not enough that people with disabilities should be accepted by their communities. Expertise must also be made available so as to enable them to be as independent as possible—which, especially in the case of children with cerebral palsy (hereafter CP), means good therapy and early intervention.

This is recognised nowadays. But the problem was that while the idea of CBR was being promoted and developed, therapists' training programmes were being starved of support. Very few new training centres were established and those that were already running were pathetically under-funded. Curricula and training material could not be renewed and morale became very low. In all the countries I lived and worked in, therapists learnt almost nothing about paediatrics in their basic training, had no models of good practice to aspire to, and had almost no continuing education courses.

The aim of the courses I ran was to start bridging the gap between the expertise of the West and the learning needs of therapists in developing countries. Western expertise in this field does not have to be high-tech. It involves good observational and analytical skills for problem-solving, and good handling and communication skills for treating and child and teaching the families to do the same. I found that the biggest difficulty in bridging this gap was that therapists, doctors and programme managers in developing countries were not easily convinced that such a seemingly simple approach could work. In the Middle East in particular, where many doctors of physical medicine were trained in former Eastern Bloc countries and believed in passive treatment modalities such as hot packs and electrotherapy for children with CP, there is still a huge reluctance to consider other approaches. On the other hand, guardians of standards in Western countries responsible for course certification and validation are understandably reluctant to make adaptations to curricula and criteria for participating in their courses. This was because they did not want to be accused of watering down standards either academically or at the level of skill acquisition.

But without changes to entry criteria, it is almost impossible for therapists from developing countries to get on to even the first rung of the ladder leading to internationally-recognised training and on-going education. Without adaptation to curricula, the courses will not prepare therapists in developing countries, either clinically or operationally, to work in their own environments. It is my belief that the need for rigorous training programmes for therapists in developing countries is overwhelming. It is in these countries that a majority of children with CP are found. It is also in these countries that therapists need the best possible training. But they will have to work differently from therapists in the West because there will never be enough resources for programmes to employ therapists at a ratio of more than 1 for every 100 children. In these circumstances, a therapist can only assess a child, plan a programme, and then teach it to family members and community workers to carry out. There can be no watering down of standards in courses that prepare therapists to work in this way, just a change of emphasis.

The aim of this book is to be a resource for therapists. It will benefit mostly those therapists who have done a practical course. My hope is that it will give a structure within which people working with children with CP can plan an effective and feasible programme for them. This structure reflects the complexities of the damage that CP causes to the central nervous system of a developing child. It also takes into account the fact that many of the people working with the children have not had opportunities to learn how to observe the children's movements and postures, or to analyse how CP interferes with these.

The structure of the book leads the reader through the process of assessing a child, planning a treatment programme and working with the family. Chapter 1 gives some theoretical background covering the development of normal movement, the way CP interferes with this and what possibilities there are to help the child overcome it. Chapter 2 is devoted entirely to observing, handling and finding out about a child in a holistic way. It encourages the reader to take note of every detail of the child's behaviour and performance. Not until Chapter 3 is he encouraged to analyse what it is that he has seen and taken note of. My idea was to break down into two separate operations the processes of observation and analysis. Chapter 4 looks at the recognition of present or threatening contractures and deformities, and discusses some ideas about prevention.

In Chapter 5, I have tried to condense into what is really much too small a space, the principles of treatment of the different kinds of CP. I know from my teaching that most people learn about principles of treatment from practical examples of how each principle can be applied. The danger with putting these examples in a book is that readers may think the examples are rigid treatment plans. This couldn't be further from the truth. I ask readers to use an example only as an illustration of *one way* in which the particular principle being explained may be applied.

Chapter 6 deals with working with families. Chapter 7 with equipment that can be useful both in therapy centres and for families to have at home. I realised I have neglected any mention of occupational therapy or speech therapy equipment. For this I apologise, but excuse myself on the grounds that in the countries I know, there are so few of these professionals that giving space in a small book such as this to describing the equipment they might need is unjustified.

However, despite the absence of the professionals themselves, there is a huge need for their expertise to be made available. That is why Chapter 8, written by Marian Browne, is devoted entirely to ways of helping children with CP to eat and drink. So many children with CP in developing countries suffer desperately from not being able to take food into their mouths, manipulate it and swallow without choking that, for many mothers, nourishing their children is their overriding concern. Marian Browne is a speech and language therapist and a Bobath Tutor. She works at the Bobath Centre in London.

My own training and practice is based on the Bobath/NDT Approach but I am not a Bobath Tutor. I have tried to practise the Approach in a way that demonstrates its benefits and convinces people of its effectiveness. I have also tried to teach the underlying skills of problem-solving and handling that allow therapists to participate in fully accredited courses. This book is a reflection only of the way in which I myself have interpreted the Approach.

Throughout this book I have used 'he' and 'she' alternately when referring to children. The same is true of therapists. I hope that readers will be able to understand, from the context, which I intend.

Causes, effects and treatment of cerebral palsy

What is Cerebral Palsy (CP)?

Cerebral means 'concerning the brain' and palsy means paralysis or the inability to move. CP then, is a kind of paralysis that results from damage to the brain. The modern definition of CP is this: A persistent, but not unchanging disorder of movement and posture* due to a non-progressive disorder of the immature (that is under 2 years of age) brain.

In other words, the damage that has been done to the child's brain cannot be cured. It is 'persistent'. The disorder of movement and posture can, however, change. It can be improved by good positioning and handling.* Conversely, it can be made worse by poor positioning and handling and by the child's use of abnormally high tone* or compensatory activities (for example, moving the head and trunk in walking when the pelvis* is stiff) in order to function.* This in turn leads to secondary contractures* and deformities* and diminishes the child's chances of being independent. The high tone also prevents muscles from growing normally, increasing the possibility of contractures.

CP is non-progressive. That is to say, the damage to the child's brain will not extend or be repeated. It is once-only event. Unfortunately, there are other rare conditions which resemble CP but which are progressive. These conditions are most often familial and can show up in more than one child in the family. Sadly, people with these progressive conditions do not live to be more than about 20. But even so, the quality of their lives and that of their families can be greatly improved by therapy.

It is important to realise what is meant by damage to an immature brain. A normal baby shows a huge variety of patterns of movement* early on in the pregnancy. Once he is born, and out of the fluid environment of the uterus, he has to learn to control and coordinate movement against the influence of gravity. He must learn to balance,* to reach out and grasp and to move from one position to another. He learns this by trial and error while his brain records the sensations of the new movements and postures. In this way, the part of his brain that controls movement and posture becomes mature.

* All words with a star against them are explained in the glossary.

The baby with CP may have been damaged early in the pregnancy and may, therefore, have abnormal movements even before birth. He too wants to learn to balance and reach and move but can only succeed in abnormal ways. His patterns of movement do not show a great variety like the normal baby's. If he has the spastic* type of CP (as opposed to the athetoid* or ataxic* type) he will have only a limited number of patterns of movement, usually not including useful ones such as reaching and grasping. Because he only experiences moving in abnormal ways, the part of his brain that controls movement is prevented from maturing. In other words, he cannot build up a store of good movement experiences that allow him to develop fine motor control.

How does it affect a child?

Main characteristics of CP

There is no space here to describe all the work that has been done on exactly how movement is controlled and coordinated by the brain and spinal cord. Briefly, voluntary and automatic learned movement is controlled by the cortex, postural control* by the basal ganglia and balance and coordination* by the cerebellum.*

If the part of the cortex that controls movement is damaged, the brain is unable to suppress the activity of the spinal cord and the muscles become stiff by constantly responding to spinal reflexes. These reflexes allow movement to happen in very limited ways—which is why a child with this kind of damage has very little variety in movement patterns. She cannot move as she likes.

This kind of stiffness is called spasticity. Spasticity is made up of two elements: neural hypertonia* and non-neural hypertonia. In neural hypertonia tone is raised because of lack of suppression from the brain; in non-neural hypertonia there is lack of elasticity in the muscles and soft tissues around the joint being moved.

If the basal ganglia are damaged, the child's tone fluctuates between low and high, sometimes severely high, because the controlling influence of the basal ganglia on the spinal cord is lost or diminished. The child will know how to move in a variety of ways but will not be able to maintain a steady position, and will have constant involuntary movements. If the cerebellum is damaged, the child can move voluntarily and maintain postures to some extent, but the coordination necessary for smooth movement and delicate balance reactions is diminished. As the child tries to balance or carry out fine motor activities, this lack of coordination shows itself as a tremor in the upper limbs or swaying in the trunk.

Children with flaccidity (hypotonia*) or very low tone are usually born prematurely. The reason for their low tone is still not fully understood but it must be the result of some failure of the development of the brain that usually occurs in the last weeks of pregnancy. It seems that damage to the basal ganglia causes a child to have low tone but many

* Cortex, basal ganglia and cerebellum are all parts of the brain.

children develop athetosis (fluctuating tone) or ataxia (intermittent tone) later when their activity brings them up against gravity.

In many children with CP, when a number of different areas of the brain may have been damaged, there is a mixture of these characteristics.

How many children are affected?

In rich countries, there are just over 2 children born with CP out of every 1,000 live births. In countries with less sophisticated medical services, the number can be as high as 1 child in every 300. In developed countries, a significant proportion of children with CP are those that are born very prematurely. In developing countries, the very premature babies do not receive the sophisticated medical intervention needed for them to survive; at the same time, lack of good antenatal and obstetric care puts more babies at risk of being born with CP. In these countries there is also a higher risk of diseases such as encephalitis and meningitis causing brain damage in very young babies, resulting in CP and associated problems such as visual, hearing and intellectual impairments.

What are the causes of CP?

In some cases, the cause of the damage is known. But in many others, it is not.

In the pre-natal period, damage may be done to the baby's brain in the following ways.

- The mother might have an infection such as German measles, shingles or even flu.
- She might take some drugs without realising they could damage her baby.
- The placenta might be insufficient. (It may be below the baby's head in the uterus where it can be easily damaged.)
- There might be incompatibility between the blood of the mother and the child (hyperbilirubinaemia).

It used to be believed that a lack of oxygen during birth caused CP, and parents often accused doctors of negligence. It has now been discovered that for most babies, the damage is likely to have taken place before birth. In these cases, the delivery may be slower because the baby cannot move normally to assist in the process, and this led to the mistaken belief that the prolonged birth was the cause of the damage and not its result.

Babies that are born prematurely or very small are susceptible to brain damage after birth. This is because the blood vessels in the brain, especially those around the ventricles, are very fragile. If those blood vessels are damaged, there can be bleeding into the ventricles, which may push outwards and damage the surrounding brain tissue. A small amount of bleeding may not result in lasting damage but a large amount certainly will.

A head injury, meningitis or encephalitis during the early years of a child's life can also cause CP.

Diagnosis

If a baby is born very premature and has difficulty breathing, it may be clear from the beginning that he has CP. This is also true of babies who sustain head injuries or who have meningitis or encephalitis. But in many cases, it is only when the baby does not develop normally that the doctor suspects CP. The baby may be abnormally floppy or rather stiff, and does not learn to sit up or reach out with her hands as other babies do. At this point the doctor must decide whether she has CP or whether the problem is one of a number of other conditions such as a tumour of the brain, a genetic or a progressive condition.

Some babies with learning difficulties are slow to learn to move and hold postures. They may not learn to sit alone until they are one year old or more. They may take a very long time to learn to walk. These children do not have CP unless they also show signs of abnormal postural tone. They will, however, benefit from therapy that will prevent them from getting stuck in each developmental stage and will encourage them to progress more quickly.

In developed countries, it is possible nowadays to look at a child's brain through a computerised tomography (CT) scan, magnetic resonance (MR) imaging and ultrasound (in a very young baby). These methods allow the doctor to see which part of the brain is damaged, or if there is a tumour that needs to be removed.

In countries where sophisticated equipment is not available, it is still possible to differentiate between some of these conditions by taking careful note of the child's development and way of moving. The problem is that this needs to be done over months, and by the time the diagnosis is made, it may be too late to intervene through surgery.

For therapists, however, the important thing is to be able to recognise abnormal postural tone no matter what the cause in the child's brain. Once abnormal postural tone is recognised, it can be changed during handling and treatment. Then the child, from a very young age, can be given opportunities to experience more normal postures and movements, helping his brain to mature. Even if he has a progressive condition, this handling and treatment will make his care easier and the quality of his life better.

Associated problems

Many children with CP do not have any other problems but unfortunately some do. Just as those parts of the brain that control posture and movement can be damaged, so too can other parts of the brain.

- The intellectual capacity of the child may be affected, making him slow to learn and understand.
- Her hearing may be affected in that she may have difficulty processing the sounds she hears. A child whose head keeps moving may find it difficult to locate or attend to sounds.
- His sight may be affected in the sense that his brain cannot perceive what the eyes see.
- Perceptual problems can lead to the child becoming fearful of moving around.
- Some children have difficulty processing sensation from their muscles and joints, and find it difficult to locate their limbs in relation to their bodies. They have to compensate by using their eyes.
- About half the children who have CP also have epilepsy. This can take a very mild form, where the child experiences temporary loss of awareness, or a severe form where the whole body shakes and the child loses consciousness for minutes at a time. These severe fits are damaging to the brain and it is important to give the child drugs that reduce the number and severity of the fits. However, drugs taken over years can also be damaging (for example, phenobarbitone can interfere with the working of the brain), and it helps to choose a drug best suited to each child.

How can therapy help?

In developed countries, most children with CP will need to see a physiotherapist, an occupational therapist and a speech therapist. The physiotherapist will work with the child to help her develop good posture and movement, the occupational therapist will look more at her function, visual perception and fine motor control, and the speech therapist will help with eating, drinking and communication. In practice, the boundaries between these three professions become blurred and there is considerable overlap and sharing of responsibilities. In developing countries, there are often no therapists and the work is done by rehabilitation assistants, teachers or anyone else who has had some training. Where there are therapists, they are most often physiotherapists who must take on the roles of occupational therapists and speech therapists as well.

With such pressure of work, it is necessary to choose priorities. For any child, the most important thing is nutrition. Before movement and posture can be worked on, the child must be able to eat and drink safely and in sufficient quantities. Physiotherapists who find themselves working alone must, therefore, be able to advise a mother on how best to feed her baby (see Chapter 8).

In the developed world, therapy for children with CP takes many forms. This reflects the fact that there is no outright 'cure' for the condition. There are several different approaches that have been devised to help the child grow and develop in the best possible way. In this book there is only space to describe these briefly. They are,

Neuro-Developmental (NDT) or Bobath Approach
This is the approach used throughout this book, and will be described in detail later in this chapter.

Conductive education
It aims to stimulate a developmental process, which will allow the child to be more easily integrated into normal education. It is carried out by conductors who combine physiotherapy, speech therapy and teaching in one programme. The children are selected and taught in groups and not all children are considered suitable. The programme was developed in Hungary by Dr Andras Peto and later Dr Maria Hari in order to allow as many children with CP as possible to learn to walk and, therefore, to attend school.

Vojta reflex locomotion
Vaclav Vojta based his treatment theory on his observation that 'global patterns of movement with components of locomotion' can be elicited in newborn babies. This led him to believe that in a child with CP, it was possible to influence the mechanism that controls body position and centre of gravity. He stimulated different points on the child's body to elicit reciprocal creeping* movements, which imprinted new muscle patterns in the central nervous system.* These can be stored and will lead to more normal spontaneous movement. Treatment is most effective when carried out on very young babies.

MOVE international curriculum
MOVE stands for Mobility Opportunities Via Education. The curriculum was developed in the United States to help learners with severe disabilities to sit, stand and walk. MOVE international is now used increasingly in Europe with children and young people and sometimes with adults.

MOVE is *not* a therapy. It is a framework for good practice that breaks down functional motor tasks into small components so that progress can be charted and motor skills practised during other educational or leisure activities. It can be used in conjunction with other therapies.

Can drugs help?

There are some drugs that can reduce spasticity. But the child becomes accustomed to them in a short time, and it will take a higher and higher dose to achieve the same result. As the dose increases, so do the side effects.

In developed countries, there has been some success with botulinum injections into the muscles. Botulinum is a very powerful toxin that works by suppressing the nerve connections to the muscle. It needs to be used with great expertise because of the high toxicity. It must always be injected in partnership with a therapist so that the maximum benefit is gained by the reduction in spasticity. The effect does not last more than 6 months, and very often there is no carry over after this time. This can leave a child and his family very disappointed and disheartened. The injection can be repeated once, but no more after that.

Perhaps the biggest benefit of trying botulinum injections is that it demonstrates the effect of surgery but is not so irreversible. So, if you want to know if a child with short tendo-achilles* will collapse into flexion* after the tendon is released, the botulinum injection will show you.

What is the Bobath (NTD) Approach and how can it help children with CP?

Dr Karel Bobath and his wife Berta Bobath began working with children with CP in the forties and continued developing the concept until they retired in 1987. They said that their concept was not so much treatment as a way of thinking about how CP can affect children. The therapist must be able to observe and analyse what it is that prevents a child from carrying out functional everyday skills, and then devise a treatment programme that will prepare the child to do these. Each child is different and must be analysed and treated in an entirely different way from any other.

Normal postural tone is the level of tension in those groups of muscles that keep us upright when gravity would pull us down. When this tone is normal, we can automatically adjust our position in a coordinated way to balance and move. It is the lack of this fine-tuned coordination that prevents children with CP from moving in functional ways and holding postures against gravity. If a child's postural tone is too high, he may be able to hold a position, but will not be able to balance or move much. If it is too low or fluctuates between low and high, he will not be able to hold a position where gravity can influence him, but he will be able to move. His movements though, will be uncoordinated and may be involuntary.

In normal movement, there is reciprocal interaction between the groups of muscles. This reciprocal interaction gives us fixation proximally* (for example, in the trunk, shoulder girdle* and pelvis) to allow for movement distally* (limbs). It gives us graded control of agonist* and antagonist.* In other words, coordinated co-contraction* for smooth timing, grading* and direction of movement. It also gives us automatic adaptation of muscles to changes in posture.

According to the Bobath Approach, the lack of normal postural control is caused by the lack of inhibition* from the central nervous system, which has been damaged as a result of the lesion. Without this inhibition, the excitation that initiates the movement cannot be changed and moulded to give coordination.

Dr and Mrs Bobath believed that children with CP could be treated if this inhibition were provided. As they worked with the children and learned from their experiences, they discovered that the best inhibition was provided by the child's own active movement.

So far, research has not been able to prove that NDT can directly affect the brain. However, the hypothesis is that by giving a young child experience of new postures and by making him active within those postures, new connections (or synapses) may be made within the brain. The more these new postures are practised, the easier they will be, and the newly connected parts of the cortex will start to suppress the spinal reflex activity.

Fundamental to the Bobath Approach is the awareness of how normal movement develops in a child. Each developmental milestone, such as holding the head erect or sitting alone, is passed only after a process of moving in certain ways and holding certain postures. For example, a new-born baby cannot hold her head erect because she has not learnt to lift it against gravity. It is only as she begins to use her eyes that she is motivated to lift her head to all positions and try to hold it steady so that she can see.

In order to learn to sit alone, the child would have gone through a very long process. This starts with her being able to hold her head erect. She must then be able to balance her trunk on her pelvis. This means having very efficient coordination between the flexion in the trunk and hips, and the extension.* The extension would have become fully developed when she lay prone* and reached for toys so that her whole body could lift off the floor. The flexion becomes fully developed through her kicking as she lies on her back, and then as she tries to catch hold of her toes and bring them to her mouth. Once flexion and extension are developed, she is ready to rotate in her trunk. She will gain this over long weeks spent in learning to roll from front to back and back to front on the floor in order to reach toys or move herself around. With this ability to coordinate flexion and extension and to rotate in the trunk comes balance reactions. Once she can sit alone and balance without using her arms for support, the whole new experience of using her hands in sitting to reach, touch and grasp objects is opened up to her.

These examples show how treatment and handling of children with CP must take into account what elements of postural control are needed before each functional goal can be achieved. Without careful analysis of what it is that is interfering with a child's ability to achieve a motor milestone or functional goal, it is not possible to plan good treatment.

How can treatment be given?

There are a few therapy centres of great excellence in some of the richer countries. These centres are a resource for teaching and research and to give examples of good practice. It is not possible or advisable for every child with CP to receive all their treatment in such centres.

In specialist centres, therapists have time to carry out long treatment sessions with each child. During these sessions, the therapist is able to use very skilled and sensitive handling techniques to enable the child to play and be active in a satisfying way. The therapist is also able to teach the child's carers to carry out similar treatment at home. All of this requires immense dedication and not every family feels ready or able to commit themselves to giving so much time and effort, not only to take the child to the centre often, but also to carry out the treatment at home.

For most children and their families, the ideal situation would be to have a centre of excellence close enough for them to visit once in a while with their therapist or whoever is helping them in treating their child. In this centre, the child would undergo a very thorough assessment so that those elements that are interfering with his functions may be clearly identified. Then a feasible programme for his handling and management can be discussed with all those caring for him. If this programme has realistic, achievable goals built into it, the family will be motivated to carry it out and come back after some months for a reassessment and a new programme.

Also, in this ideal centre, specialist doctors could see children from time to time to assess their medical needs. Those children who need medication to prevent seizures, for example, need regular monitoring, and many children need to have x-rays and be seen by orthopaedic specialists to check they are not in danger of hip dislocation and other deformities. Alongside these services, there could also be orthotic experts to provide appropriate splints, psychologists to help families with learning disabilities and behaviour problems, perhaps a toy library to encourage interesting play, and a workshop where special equipment such as chairs or standing frames could be made.

This kind of a centre would be a resource for community-based rehabilitation programmes to call upon. The role of the experts based in such a centre would be to advise the community workers when they need help in order to progress with a particular child. They would also be able to monitor children's progress particularly in the years when they are growing fast and are, therefore, in greater danger of contractures and deformities.

When such centres are not possible because there are no highly qualified experts, there is still a good deal that can be done for children with CP by community workers or volunteers who are ready to learn and who are convinced that something worthwhile can be done.

The most important thing for any child with CP is to have opportunities to socialise with other children in the family and in the community. To do this, the child needs to be placed in positions other than lying. Community workers who have the possibility of working with carpenters or who can make pieces of cardboard equipment (Appropriate Paper-based Technology or APT) for positioning children, can make a huge difference to the children they work with.

Challenges for people working with children with CP

To encourage acceptance and hope
The fact that CP causes damage to a child's brain that cannot be reversed or cured is very hard for everyone concerned to come to terms with. The doctors, therapists, community workers and others working with the child and her family have a narrow path to walk. They must help those closest to the child to find a balance between, on the one hand, acceptance of the child as she is and, on the other, the hope that she can be helped to be more independent. Without acceptance that the child's disability is part of her like the colour of her hair or the size of her nose, there will always be a sense of failure and disappointment. But acceptance does not mean resignation. Acceptance must be accompanied by hope that, despite difficulties, she can achieve some or even full independence,

that she can take some or total control over her life and that there are proven ways and means of achieving this. The challenge for the professionals working with families is to recognise that each family finds the balance between these two things in their own way. It is a process that cannot be hurried. But families can be encouraged to have realistic hope, and they can be sympathetically supported as they find it within themselves to accept their child's condition.

To ensure adequate resources
Lack of sophisticated equipment and expensive aids does not have to mean that good services cannot be provided. Children need well designed chairs and standing frames, but these can be made out of cheap materials. Local carpenters and metal workers can make good quality pieces if they are given good design. In many programmes, parents themselves learn to make equipment for their children out of cardboard and paper (APT). This activity gives parents a very positive view of their ability to help their child, and they can later train other parents.

To provide ongoing training programmes
There is a great need for programmes throughout the world for training all professional and non-professional people working with children with CP. Well-trained therapists can lift a programme up so that everyone can see good results and spread the message of realistic hope mentioned earlier. The expertise that is available in rich countries must be made available everywhere. Once the expertise is available, it can be adapted and made appropriate for different cultures, and each country can set up its own sustainable ongoing training programme. Standards can then be maintained and strong cross-cultural links forged through exchanging of ideas and sharing of information internationally.

To provide good management
Working with children with CP has to be a team effort. No one person can achieve good results. Good management is the key to keeping the team working well.

The manager may be a doctor or an administrator. The title is not important, but the role that he or she plays as a leader who respects all team members equally and inspires them to achieve good results is crucial. Managers can ensure good working conditions for team members even if the pay cannot be good, they can counsel team members who are struggling and acknowledge good work, they can manage resources efficiently, and they can represent the work of the programme to the outside world.

Most of all, a good manager sees the work of the programme as a whole within the context of the community, and ensures that the best possible service is provided within the constraints of available resources. This can only be done by being very close to all the team members and parents, and listening to and empathising with their views and concerns.

2

Assessment of children with cerebral palsy–Collecting information

The assessment of a child with CP is the key to good treatment. Each child with CP is different and the therapist treating the child must be able to find out the underlying causes of his or her inability to function normally before the treatment can be effective.

To give an example, a child with spastic quadriplegia can perhaps sit alone on the floor when placed, but her balance reactions seem not to be reliable and she is fearful of falling. It might seem reasonable, in this case, for the therapist to work to develop better balance reactions, but in fact this will not succeed unless the spasticity* around the child's hips and pelvis* is first reduced. A good assessment would reveal that this spasticity is the cause of the child's inability to learn to balance well.

Figure 2.1

This little girl can sit alone on the floor but the spasticity in her hips prevents her from balancing and from being able to use her hands to play.

I have devoted two chapters in this small book to assessment because it is so important and because there are so many things to consider and understand if you are to do a good job.

Each assessment needs to be broken down into three steps.

First, learn about the child through observation and handling, and by listening to the family's account of how she functions at home.

Second, analyse your observations and the information received from the family and create a full written record. During this process, you will decide which type of CP the child has, in what way her postural tone is abnormal, and which abnormal patterns she mostly uses to function.

Third, conclude your analysis by working out what major problems are preventing the child from being able to function well. This will provide the foundation for an effective treatment plan.

In this chapter, I will describe how to gather the information needed, giving you a step-by-step guide to observing and handling the child you are assessing.

The second and third steps of the assessment—the analysis and conclusions—will be dealt with in Chapter 3.

Observing the child

While you are observing him, you want the child to enjoy getting to know you and perhaps to be interested in the toys you have for him to play with.

You will want to observe him

sitting on a family member's knee (if he is a small child),
sitting on a stool with feet flat on the floor,
sitting on the floor,
supine* on the floor,
prone on the floor,
held in standing or alone, if he can, and
changing from one position to another (sequences of movement).

In all these positions you will be watching the child to see:

- **How much support he needs.** Take note of where the family member places his or her hands on the child. Does the child's head need support all the time? If the trunk is supported, can the child support his head by himself? The family member's support of the child, or the lack of it, will tell you a good deal about the child's abilities to move and maintain postures against gravity.

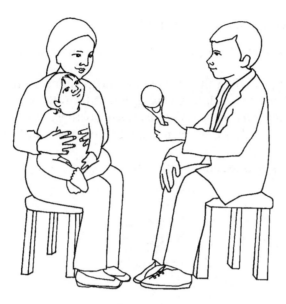

Figure 2.2

As the therapist observes the child on her mother's knee and listens to the mother's account, the child is deciding whether or not to trust the therapist.

- **How much movement there is.** Is it too much or too little? Normal young children who are in a wakeful state are constantly moving, but in a way that leads to more functional and purposeful activities as they experiment and explore their environment. A child with spasticity or a child with very low tone will not show this kind of movement. His movement may be laboured or even absent. There are also children whose movement is too much, and this interferes with their ability to come up against gravity and to stay there. Finally, there are children who can move, but because of sensory or perceptual problems, they become distressed and fearful when they are moved or attempt to move on their own.
- **The quality of movement.** Is it normally smooth and appropriate for the child's age? Or is it jerky and in uncoordinated, non-functional patterns? Is it slow and laboured and limited in its range? Is there an intention tremor when the child attempts a function?
- **What abilities (function) the child has, regardless of whether or not they are carried out normally.** By function, we mean the child's ability to hold himself and to move in a number of different positions such as sitting alone or bearing weight on his legs in standing. Does he have balance reactions and protective responses? Can he coordinate a large variety of movements and carry out activities that are appropriate for his age, that allow him to play and explore his environment as he wants?

- **Pathological symptoms.** These could be:

  1. *Involuntary movements,* i.e., movements that occur when the child does not intend them.
  2. *Asymmetry,** i.e., when the movement and position of the head influences one side of the body to work in a way different from the other.
  3. *Stereotyped abnormal patterns of movement.* If these are constantly used, and if they are seen with an abnormal quality of postural tone, they are certainly pathological.
  4. *Moro reaction,* or frequent startle responses.

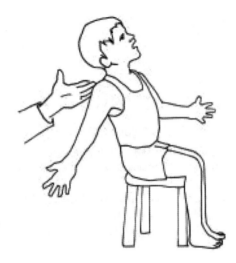

Figure 2.3

The Moro reaction occurs when a child feels his head is falling back. His arms abduct and outwardly rotate, his hands and mouth open wide. He would fall if not supported.

- **How the child behaves.** You will need to record how fearful the child is of strangers or a strange situation. But, equally, you will need to record if he is interested in what is going on. If he likes a particular book or a toy, or if he enjoys social play more than toys. Do his responses give you indications of how well he is able to see and hear? Can he follow an object to all sides with his eyes? Does he turn towards a sound?

Besides these general observations, there are specific things to look for and test as the child moves or is placed in each of the following positions.

Young child sitting on a family member's knee

This is usually the first position in which you will see the child. It is a chance for you to observe her while she feels secure. She will, of course, also be assessing you to see if she can trust you, so give her time before going too close.

What you will want to observe in this position is,

- Does she try to hold herself upright, or does she need support? Where and how does the family member give her this support?
- How much does she move? Which part of her body moves? Which part stays still?
- How much does she use her hands? If she is shy to take a toy from you, give it to the family member first and see whether the child will try to reach out for it.

While you are observing these things, you can spend time to ask the family member about the child at home. Listen carefully so that you can form a clear picture, not only of what the child can do but *how* she does it. You will also want to find out how the family copes and what their feelings are about the child. Ask the following questions:

- What is the child's medical and family history?
- What positions is the child put in at home for playing, feeding, sleeping, washing, dressing and carrying?
- Are there difficulties with eating and drinking?
- How does she communicate?
- Are there difficulties in hearing and vision?
- What is the family's main problem in caring for her?

Child sitting on a stool with feet flat on the floor

If the child is not able to sit alone, ask the family member to show you how they would normally place her on the stool and hold her. What you will want to observe in this position is:

- Where, if at all, is the support needed?
- Is the child's head and trunk in alignment* or is there asymmetry?
- Does she sit back on her sacrum,* or can she support her trunk on her pelvis with her hips flexed at a right angle?
- Can she reach outside her base without losing balance—for example, reach down to the floor or out to one side?

- Does she have saving reactions?
- How well can she use her hands in this position? Does she need to use them for support or balance?

Child sitting on the floor

With the child in long sitting* on the floor, you should look at the following:

- Alignment of head on trunk, trunk on pelvis and pelvis on legs. Is the child sitting back on her sacrum?
- Is there head and trunk control?
- Does she balance well?
- Is her weight distributed equally on both sides?
- Do her legs adjust as she reaches out with her arms?
- Can she take weight on straight arms?
- Can she use her hands, or does she need them for support?
- Does she mostly sit on the floor between her legs which are flexed and inwardly rotated* (W-sitting)?

Figure 2.4

Some children find they can use their hands more easily in W-sitting.

Figure 2.5

A child who cannot flex well enough at his hips sits back on his sacrum when
his knees are straight, and has to compensate with a good deal of
flexion in his upper trunk. This makes his arms flex more.

Child supine on the floor

When the child is placed in this position you will want to observe:

- If the child is in alignment, i.e., head in the middle, not pushing back into extension
  or turning to one side all the time, trunk straight, legs mostly symmetrical.*

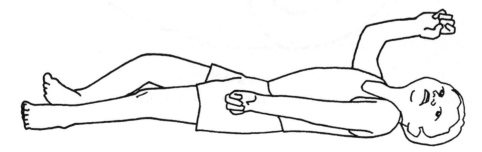

Figure 2.6

This child shows asymmetry and he is pushing back into extension.

- What movements he makes in his head and limbs. Can he bring his hands together in front of his eyes?
- Does he kick with his legs? Is the movement symmetrical? Does he kick reciprocally?
- Can he lift his head off the floor?
- Does he try to roll?

Child prone on the mat

If it is difficult to get the child into this position or if she becomes very distressed, leave this position for a later date. If she tolerates the position, you will want to observe:

- Can she lift her head against gravity and turn it to either side?
- Can she take weight on her forearms and reach out with either hand, or are her arms trapped under her body?
- Can she take weight when placed on extended arms? Can she push up herself on to extended arms?
- In what position are her legs?
- Are her head and trunk in alignment?

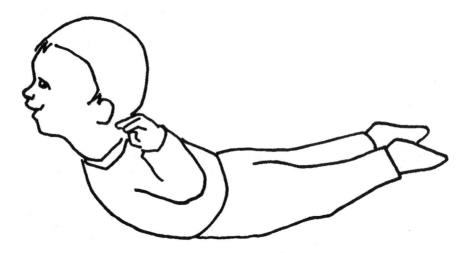

Figure 2.7

A normal baby of about 6 months can lift all limbs as well as his head and trunk against gravity.

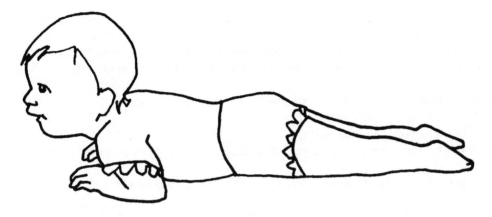

Figure 2.8

A child with flexor spasticity in prone can only just lift her head.

Child held in standing

Even if a child is totally unable to take weight on her legs, it is important for you to see what happens when she is held in standing. You, or the family member, should hold her

Figure 2.9

This child shows asymmetry with abnormal pattern of flexion, adduction and inward rotation of the hips, and plantarflexion* of the feet. The arms are in abnormal flexion, inward rotation and pronation.

in alignment with her hips over her feet and her knees straight. Most normal children over 7 months and most children with CP enjoy being placed in standing and respond by pushing against the ground with their feet. You will need to record if the child you are assessing does not respond in this way. You will also want to observe:

- If her legs show abnormal patterns of movement or posture.
- If she has active extension in her hips.
- If her legs collapse into flexion.
- If she has involuntary stepping (an inability to keep both feet on the ground).

If a child is able to stand, perhaps holding with one or two hands, you will want to see:

- How much does she need her hands for balance or support?
- Do her feet react normally to taking her body weight?
- Does she hold with a good grip?
- Does she have active extension in her hips?
- Do her knees hyperextend?

Sequences of movement

By sequences of movement we mean the way the child moves from one position to another. In order to do this, the child must have some of the following:

- coordinated rotation* in the trunk,
- the ability to bear weight on mobile limbs,
- head and trunk control, and
- balance reactions.

Severely affected children may not be able to move out of any position in which they are placed. Others may be able to move in and out of positions, but in an abnormal way. Still others may get stuck, especially at the point where they must come up against gravity.

As you watch the child change his position, you will need to observe how he is compensating for his difficulties.

The following sequences are the most useful ones for you to observe a child carrying out. As she tries to do each one, you must take notice of where she is getting stuck. Help her just enough so that she can continue with the movement.

- *Rolling from prone to supine and supine to prone over either side*
- *Sitting up from supine over either elbow*
- *Changing from sitting to crawling* position*
- *Crawling*

- *Pull to standing* from crawling position*
- *Pull to standing from sitting on a stool*
- *Stepping sideways while holding on (cruising)*
- *Stepping forward with support*
- *Walking with hands/hand held*
- *Walking unaided*

In each sequence, there are different observations to be made. We will take each of them in turn.

Rolling from prone to supine

Normal rolling from prone to supine involves being able to turn the head to one side, to rotate and extend the trunk, first lifting either one shoulder or one leg off the floor, then to twist around the body axis in a controlled way over the arm caught underneath the body, to finally lie supine.

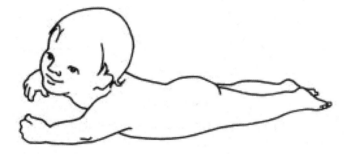

Figure 2.10a

Head turns to side.

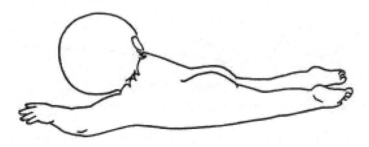

Figure 2.10b

Head and trunk extend and rotate.

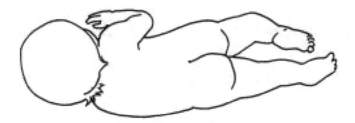

Figure 2.10c

Arm rises and trunk rotates further.

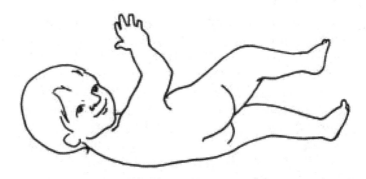

Figure 2.10d

Leg lifts off the floor and head rotates further.

Figure 2.10e

Arm caught under the trunk is released as child controls final move into supine.

The child you are assessing may be able to roll from prone to supine but not in the normal way. Usually, the problem is that there is very little rotation, and in order to come into supine, the child must use her head to initiate total extension and flick herself over. A second child may curl into flexion and roll with her knees bent up or propped on bent arms so she is not lying flat.

Many children can roll into supine over only one side. It is important to record which. A child may get stuck in trying to roll from prone to supine in several ways, as can be seen in the following drawings.

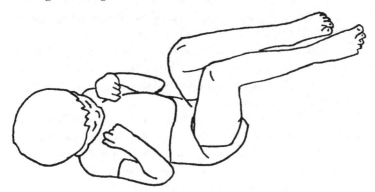

Figure 2.11

Head and shoulder girdle strongly flexed.

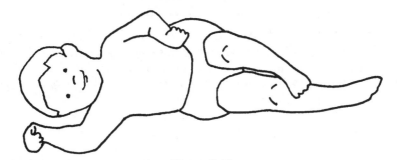

Figure 2.12

Arm trapped awkwardly when child rolls to side.

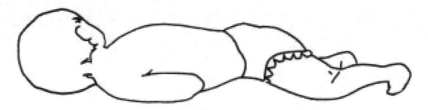

Figure 2.13

Hips strongly flexed and abducted.

Rolling from supine to prone

Normally, a child will initiate rolling from supine to prone by turning her head and may be reaching across her body with an arm. It is equally normal though, to initiate rolling by bringing one leg across. In either case, a normal child will find herself in side lying,* from where she may, by lifting and turning her head, roll into prone. In order to do this smoothly and without discomfort, the child must be able to adjust the arm underneath, so that it does not become trapped in an awkward position. Because she is able to extend and rotate her head and trunk, she will be able shift her weight off the trapped arm.

A child who lies in supine with her arms widely abducted and outwardly rotated* at the shoulders and flexed at the elbows, cannot roll over without coming up on one elbow or causing pain at the shoulder joint.

When you ask the child you are assessing to roll over, it helps to first ask her to follow a toy with her eyes. Move the toy so that she turns her head to one side and then extends it. Show her where you are placing the toy and encourage her to roll to reach it. Watch carefully to see how she rolls over. Is it like a log, or does she have some rotation in her trunk? Does she sit up rather than roll into prone? Can she roll over one side only? If she can't complete the roll, take careful note of her difficulties. In what part of the sequence is she getting stuck? Which part of her body is causing the problem?

Sitting up from supine over either elbow

In order to do this, a child must be able to lift his head off the floor, shift his weight on to one side (rotation of the trunk), take weight on his flexed arm and push up into sitting. This sequence comes late in a normal child's motor development (after about 9 months). As you watch the child attempting to do this, note at which point he has difficulty. Is it easier on one side than the other?

Changing from sitting on the floor to crawling position

This involves the child being able to shift weight on to one side and take weight on both arms to one side of her body while maintaining her balance (mobile weight bearing).* Using her arms as a pivot, she then has to rotate her trunk and lift her pelvis over her flexed knees to come up into all fours kneeling. Where does she have difficulty? Is it better over one side than the other? Can she reverse the sequence and come back into sitting again?

Figure 2.14

Normal coming up to sitting, with weight bearing on one arm and rotation in trunk.

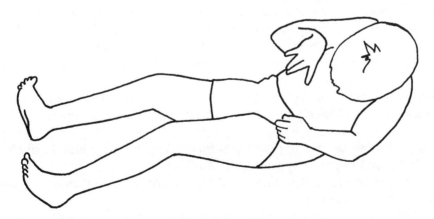

Figure 2.15

Failure to come to sitting because no weight bearing on arm,
no rotation in trunk and not enough hip flexion.

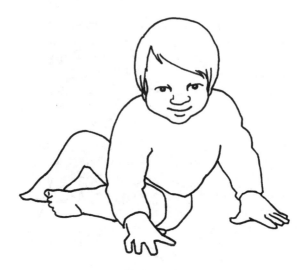

Figure 2.16

In this sequence of movement, the child's arms are fully extended while her legs are flexed.
She has to balance her weight on her arms, rotate her trunk and bring her knees into
position under her hips so that she can take weight on them.

Crawling

Most normal children learn to move around the floor on hands and knees (crawling). In
order to crawl normally, a child needs rotation in her trunk and mobile weight-bearing
on all her limbs to allow her to take weight on each one in turn. She also needs to be able
to support herself on legs bent at right angles at the hips and knees, and on arms with
straight elbows. Then she needs to be able to move her arms and legs reciprocally and
shift her weight from side to side.

Some children with CP can crawl, but in an abnormal way. The following are some of
the abnormal ways in which you may see the child you are assessing crawl:

- Bunny hopping, or, moving both legs forward at the same time in the way that a
  rabbit (bunny) hops along (see Figure 3.18).
- With very short steps, with knees and hips flexed to more than a right angle—not
  good enough extension.
- Children who have difficulty balancing in four-point kneeling will often crawl with
  their legs quite widely abducted and flexed.
- With asymmetry, i.e., with more weight and better steps on one side than the other.
- With most of the weight over arms, and legs dragging.

Some normal children choose not to crawl, and instead move around the floor in sitting. This is called bottom shuffling. Those children with CP who are more affected on one side than the other will sometimes bottom shuffle in side-sitting. They will pull themselves along using one hand and pushing with the leg on the same side. You will need to take note of the side on which the child side-sits on.

Figure 2.17

Bottom shuffling using only one side.
Other side is strongly retracted.

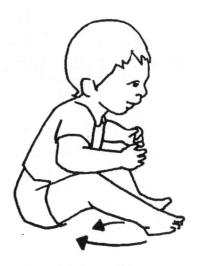

Figure 2.18

Symmetrical bottom shuffling
using a lot of flexion.

Other children with CP might bottom shuffle symmetrically, but you will need to look at their sitting postures and note how they are using their legs and arms as they move around.

Pull to standing from crawling position

A child will normally do this at around 9 months of age. She will come up into high kneeling grasping the edge of a chair, for example, bring one leg forward into half kneeling,* and then push on the forward leg and pull with her arms to come up into standing. Most normal children will prefer to use one leg to push themselves up on rather than the other, but they *can* use either leg.

You should note where the child you are assessing is having difficulty, or where she uses abnormal patterns. She may, for example, have very little dissociation* between her legs, and may pull them both into extension at the same time as she drags her weight up over her legs using strong flexion in her arms. She may take most of the weight on her arms and very little on her legs. She may have involuntary movements that interfere with her ability to organise the sequence.

Figure 2.19

Arms strongly pulling leads to spasticity in legs. One leg is then
not able to move in a different pattern to the other.

Pull to standing from sitting on a stool

A normal child who stands up from sitting on a stool will first shift her weight forward, bringing her head almost in front of her feet. This brings her centre of gravity forward and makes it easy for her to use her legs to push up into standing. She does not need to use her hands at all.

Children with spasticity may use their arms to perform the function, and pull themselves up with a good deal of flexion of the arms while the legs extend in a spastic pattern. You should note if the child can take weight equally on her legs as she pulls into standing. Child with fluctuating tone may be able to stand up, but will have poor balance and may not be able to stand still.

Stepping sideways while holding on (cruising)

For all normal children learning to walk, this is an important preparation because they are learning to balance on one leg while moving the other. In order to be able to do this, they have to first hold with one hand while weight-bearing on one leg; they then have to balance the trunk and pelvis over the leg, and shift the other leg and other hand sideways into abduction.* Many children with CP will have difficulty in doing this. They may manage in an abnormal way, with flexion at the hip for instance, or up on their toes. They may not be able to hold the pelvis steady, or they may be able to step in one direction and not the other because the pelvis is fixed.

Stepping forward with support

A normal child taking her first step with her hand held will do so with her legs abducted and outwardly rotated. Her trunk will sway sideways a little because she does not yet have fully coordinated rotation in her trunk and hips. She will waddle. Children with CP are often taught to step forward holding on to a walking aid, but they may do so by holding the pelvis rigid and using flexion and extension of the trunk to compensate for the lack of movement in the pelvis. Their steps will be small, their balance poor and as they get tired, this will become worse. You may notice that they can take bigger steps with one leg than with the other.

Children who have asymmetry and involuntary movements in their arms may not be able to hold on with their hands, but may be able to take steps if they are supported at the pelvis.

Walking unaided

Children with hemiplegia,* moderate diplegia,* mild quadriplegia and ataxia are most likely to be able to walk unaided. Many athetoid children learn to walk unaided, often at a late age. All have different problems, and the way they compensate for their difficulties may often put them in danger of contractures and deformities. That is why it is important for you to observe how the child is walking, what difficulties she has and how she is compensating for them.

The following are some of the features of a child's gait that you will need to observe:

- Are there good balance reactions and protective responses?
- Are the child's feet widely separated, or are they close together?
- Is there equal weight distribution on each leg?
- What touches the ground first, the heel or the toes?
- Are the steps taken by either leg of equal length?
- Does the child have to move the head and trunk more than is normal to compensate for stiffness around the pelvis?
- Do the child's arms get stiffer as he walks for longer?
- Can the child stop when asked to?
- Can the child change direction while walking?

The following are some examples of compensatory activities:

- Some children give themselves stability by holding the pelvis rigid. In order to move and take steps, they must then flex and extend the trunk in an exaggerated way.

- Some children may walk with too much flexion in their knees and hips (crouch gait). In order to keep upright, they must arch the lower part of their back.
- Some children with poor stability learn to stand and walk by holding their hands together. This gives them a fixed point from which to move.

This completes the section on observation. Of course, it is not possible to describe every detail of how a child might hold different postures and move. But I hope this section has given you some guidelines on the sort of thing you could record and use in your analysis of the child's problems.

Handling the child

Through observation, we record patterns of movement and posture. We see how a child functions and how she compensates for incomplete function. But in order to find out more about the underlying causes of the problems and abnormalities that we see, we must feel with our hands the degrees of change in tension in the child as she moves and makes efforts to function in different postural patterns. We must also test the range of movement in the child's joints by handling them.

Assessment and treatment go hand in hand. When we find stiffness, floppiness or instability, it should be a part of our assessment to see how easily and quickly the child can respond to the changes that we make or the support that we give.

Postural tone

The main characteristic of CP is abnormal postural tone. If a child's postural tone is normal, she will have enough tension and readiness in her muscles to allow her to hold herself in a wide range of positions even where gravity might cause her to fall. Her normal tone will also allow her to carry out coordinated functional movements without effort. If we move one of her limbs, we will find that it feels light and there is neither too little nor too much resistance to the movement. The child with normal tone will help us to move her limb smoothly.

Moving a part of the child's body, then, is a good test for us to find out the state of tension (or the tone) in her muscles. We will want to do this in a variety of different positions and take note of when there is more or less resistance to our efforts.

We will also want to see if, by positioning and handling the child in certain ways, we can change the tone quality.

In sitting

While the child is sitting, alone or supported, either on the floor or on a stool, you can feel the tone in his arms and shoulder girdle.

If his tone is lower than normal, you will feel little resistance as you raise each arm in turn over his head with his elbow either bent or straight. You will feel his whole limb to be heavy, and his joints will allow you to move his arm in a greater range than normal. His elbows may hyperextend, his wrist and fingers extend more than is normal. His shoulder and shoulder girdle will feel quite loose.

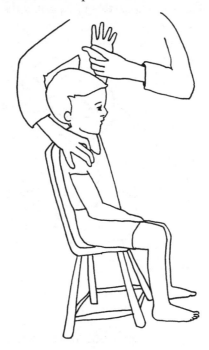

Figure 2.20

Lifting up a child's arm helps the therapist feel what the tension in the muscles is like.

We can try to change abnormally low tone by placing the child, still in sitting, so that she is bearing weight on her extended arm on a table in front of her. We can help her to bear weight on her arms by holding her elbows straight and stimulating her by talking to her or getting her to follow a toy with her eyes. The secret of good handling is then to withdraw support, even if only for a second, so that she holds the position herself. As soon as she begins to collapse, your hands must be ready to support her again.

If her tone is high, you will find resistance while trying to move her arm.

If her abnormal pattern is predominantly flexion, when you raise her arm you will feel that she is pulling against you into adduction* and inward rotation. At the same time, you may notice increased extensor tone* in her legs so that her hips extend a little and her bottom slides forward on the stool.

If the abnormal pattern in her arms and trunk is predominantly extension, you will probably be able to lift her arm to shoulder height but this may put her in danger of falling backwards. You may feel resistance when you try to bring her arm down and extend her elbows.

If her tone is fluctuating, you may, as you move the arm, feel it to be heavy and easily moved, but you may also feel a range of sudden tone changes. These tone changes will interfere with your efforts to move the limb smoothly.

It is part of assessment to see if we can change these abnormal patterns. By taking away one or two elements of the typical pattern, we break the pattern up.* This is where treatment and assessment overlap.

Figure 2.21

Part of the assessment is trying out what happens when we change something. Here, the therapist flexes and outwardly rotates the child's hips to see if it will help him to get better flexion in his hips at the same time as actively reaching forward with his arms and extending his trunk.

So, briefly, during assessment, we try out some changes in the child's position to find out how he responds, and also if this might improve his ability to function. Much more about how to break up patterns of spasticity will be found in Chapter 5.

For example, a child who sits on the floor with his weight back on his sacrum, his hips somewhat extended, adducted and inwardly rotated, cannot balance well or easily use his hands. To change this, we can try to bring his trunk forward over his legs so that his hips are flexed but his knees are still extended. We can abduct and outwardly rotate his hips a little and help him to actively use his arms to reach up and out. If this is too difficult, it may be better to try the same activity sitting on a low stool.

We want to see how well he accommodates to this kind of handling, and also want to find out if the same activity would be worthwhile and feasible for a family member to do at home.

In supine

Try lifting his head off the mat. Do you feel resistance? Turn his head to one side and hold it there. Wait a few seconds to see if he flexes his arm and leg on the side away from his face. If he does, he has asymmetric tonic neck reflex (ATNR).

Asymmetric tonic neck reflex is seen when a child's head is turned to one side and this brings about flexion in the child's opposite arm and sometimes leg. There is also extension in the arm and leg on the side to which the child's face is turned. A child with ATNR may have difficulty in maintaining his head in midline while moving his eyes to the side. He may be unable to bring both hands together in midline, especially in supine.

Move his arms slowly in all directions to feel if there is resistance. Is there, for example, spasticity in the shoulder girdle that holds his shoulders and arms in retraction and makes it difficult to bring his hands together in midline?

Figure 2.22

Holding the child's head turned to one side for a few
seconds will show if he has ATNR.

If he is crying and voluntarily resisting, wait for a chance to try when he is less distressed.

Hold his hands and pull him slowly to sitting. If he is very floppy hold his arms at the elbows. Does his head fall back? When he is sitting, talk to him keeping eye contact. Slowly lower him to lying again and note at what point he can no longer prevent his head from falling back.

In prone

If the child cannot come up on his elbows, try placing him in that position. Notice how difficult this is. Does he seem to want to pull his arms under his body all the time? Is the tone too low around the shoulder girdle for him to hold himself up? If any of these activities in prone are too difficult, try placing him over a rolled-up blanket or over your leg so that his elbows are on the ground and his chest is supported. Can he tolerate this? Can he lift his head and turn it? Try getting him to use his hands to grasp a toy in this position. Is his back actively extending, even if only momentarily?

A child who has intermittent spasms is most likely to have them while he lies prone. Note if these are a problem to him. (They are usually uncomfortable.) You will be aware of them when his hips suddenly come up off the mat and his head pulls into flexion. If they occur, see if you can prevent them by pressing down firmly on his sacrum and rocking him very slightly from side to side.

Figure 2.23

The therapist is finding out if the child can actively extend his head
and trunk in prone if he is given help. In this case, his trunk is
already lifted up, and he has fixation on his pelvis.

Sequences of movement

There is no room in such a small book to describe how you can help a child carry out all possible sequences of movement. The principle is to use your hands to give the child stability where he needs it, in order to help him have a fixed point from which to move. You then use key points of control* to facilitate* movement and change of position. For example, if you want to help a small child to push up into standing from sitting, have him sit on your knees with his feet flat on the floor. Hold his two knees with one of your hands. Support his trunk with the other. Push down through the hand holding his knees (stability) while tipping his whole body forward so that his head is ahead of his feet. Tell him to stand up. Most children, if they are put in this position, love to push into standing. Wait to see if he can actively push up; then help him to complete the action. When he is in standing, use your body to facilitate extension in his hips and hold his body in alignment. Keep him actively reaching up with enjoyment so that he is further facilitated to actively extend.

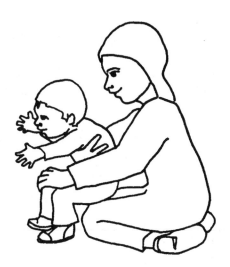

Figure 2.24

The therapist uses one hand to press down through the child's knees. With the other hand, she supports his trunk and helps him to bring his head forward just in front of his feet. He will then be in a good position to try to push up into standing.

Figure 2.25

Once he has pushed up a little by himself, the therapist supports him with her body, making sure that his hips are in good extension and his body in alignment. She then assesses if he can actively extend his hips, knees and trunk in this position.

This chapter has described all the different ways in which you can find out as much as possible about how much a child with CP can do, and how. It has also given you some idea of how to find out what he might be able to do if he has the right kind of help. If your findings are detailed enough and well recorded, you will be able to analyse them and discover the underlying causes of the child's problems with posture and movement.

3

Assessment of children with cerebral palsy–
Analysis of information

This chapter will guide you through the process of making a record of what you have observed. The object is not just to store the information but also to analyse it, leading to an assessment of the causes behind the child's problems. You could use the following headings as a framework for your report:

> *Diagnosis (Which kind of CP)*
> *History*
> *Family's concerns* (see Chapter 6)
> *General impression*
> *Abilities*
> *Inabilities*
> *Basic tone*
> *Postural patterns*
> *Contractures and deformities*
> *Main underlying problems*

In the first section of this chapter you will learn how the different kinds of CP are classified. Matching the observations you have made about the child you are assessing with the features of each kind of CP given will help you diagnose which kind of CP the child has.

The second section deals with all the other information you need to consider, put under headings that will make it easy for you to record and think about.

The third section helps you to use all the information and knowledge gathered in the first two sections to understand what might be the underlying causes of the child's problems.

Section 1

Diagnosis (Which kind of CP)

The different types of CP can be described under two main headings: the parts of the body affected and the quality of the child's postural tone.

A child whose body is affected totally is called a quadriplegia, one whose lower limbs are mostly affected is a diplegia and one whose upper and lower limb on one side is affected is a hemiplegia.

A young child with diplegia may also show some spasticity in her arms and trunk but these parts will be much less affected. Also, one side of her body will be more affected than the other. In contrast, in a child with quadriplegia, the whole body will be affected. In a young child, the arms and shoulder girdle often have spasticity while the legs seem rather immobile and primitive (see definitions). As the child gets older and tries to come up against gravity, the spasticity is seen in the legs too.

Deciding on the quality of tone is the next task. A child with CP will have one of the following kinds of abnormal tone:

severely spastic or moderately spastic,
athetoid,
ataxic,
flaccid, or
mixed (e.g., athetoid with spasticity)

Once you have decided what kind of tone the child has, you can describe the category of CP he has. He may be quadriplegic athetoid or spastic hemiplegia, for example. Look at the boxes on the following pages and compare the notes you made about the child's tone with the features described for each type of abnormal tone.

Features of severe spasticity

Exaggerated co-contraction.
Tone unchanging with changing conditions.
Tone increased proximally more than distally.
Very little or no movement.
Movement only in middle range.
Difficulty in initiating movement.
Difficulty in adjusting to being moved or handled.
No balance or protective reactions.*
Poor righting reactions.*
Associated reactions* causing increased spasticity not seen as movements.

Severe spasticity can be seen in a child who is a quadriplegia, a diplegia or a hemiplegia.

Figure 3.1

Child with severe spasticity.

Exaggerated co-contraction means that flexors and extensors (or agonists and antagonists) are equally spastic. So, there will be resistance to moving the child's limb in any direction.

When a child with severe spasticity tries to move, or when he is handled and moved, he can become very flexed or very extended.

Figure 3.2

Child with severe spasticity in total extension pattern.

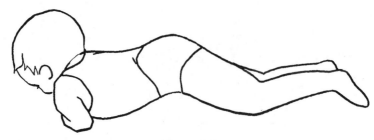

Figure 3.3

Child with severe spasticity in total flexion pattern.

Features of moderate spasticity

Changeable hypertonus rising from relatively normal at rest to high or very high with stimulation, effort, speech or emotion (particularly fear).

Poor balance and protective responses.

Spasticity more distal than proximal.

Associated reactions, seen as movements, likely to increase spasticity as child uses effort to function.

Child likely to move and function using stereotyped abnormal patterns.

Total patterns of flexion or extension which are likely to be compensatory, i.e., flexion in lower limbs with extension in upper and vice versa.

A child with moderate spasticity will move about and be able to do some things for himself, but mostly with abnormal patterns and a good deal of effort. Compensatory

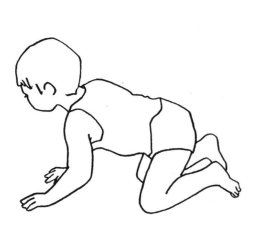

Figure 3.4

A child with moderate spasticity using flexor spasticity to move.

Figure 3.5

A child with moderate spasticity using extensor spasticity to move.

spastic patterns, where flexion in one part of the body compensates for extension in another (and vice versa) are characteristic. This is seen, for example, when a child uses flexion in her arms and trunk to pull herself along the floor in prone, her legs stiffly extend and adduct. Or a child with legs adducted and stiffly extended while trying to stand, whose arms and upper trunk are held in the abnormal pattern of flexion.

Features of athetosis

Constant fluctuations in tone between abnormally high and abnormally low.
Involuntary movements.
Lack of adequate co-contraction leading to difficulty in sustaining postural control against gravity, and poor proximal fixation.
Inadequate balance and protective responses.
Marked asymmetry.
Lack of grading of movement.
Child dislikes being held still.

A child with athetosis moves constantly, but not in a purposeful way. He has no stability, particularly in his head and trunk so that it seems as if his limbs are suspended on loose strings. He also has a problem in getting his head, hands and eyes to come to midline and stay there. Lack of grading of movement means that he cannot smoothly control a movement through a range. He can shoot from full flexion in a joint to full extension.

Figure 3.6

His ATNR makes it difficult for him
to keep his head in midline.

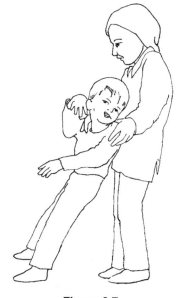

Figure 3.7

An athetoid child loves to take steps but he
lacks the co-contraction to hold himself steady.

This is particularly true of children who become stuck in extreme positions and must wait for several minutes or longer before they can move out of the position. The marked asymmetry that is a characteristic of athetoids is one of their most disabling features. An athetoid child has great difficulty holding her head in midline. Since the head position in these children determines the postural patterns in the rest of the body, any movement of the head causes involuntary movements in all the limbs.

Features of ataxia

Postural tone is fairly low to normal. The child can move and hold some postures against gravity.
Co-contraction is poor, causing difficulty in holding steady postures.
Proximal fixation is not effective for carrying out selective movements.
There may be an intention tremor and jerky quality of movement, especially with effort and against gravity.
Inadequate balance reactions and slow or delayed protective responses.
Poor grading of movement.

The picture of a child with ataxia is of a child with poor balance, who can function fairly well but with a poor quality of posture and movement, especially when he is up against gravity. His posture and movement is distinguished by shakiness, by a slowness to react and by seeming to come from a wobbly base.

Figure 3.8

An ataxic child has poor postural control because of
intermittent tone. She also has poor balance.

Features of flaccidity or hypotonus (low tone)

Child takes up all available support.
Poor head and trunk control.
Child doesn't move much.
Joints are hypermobile (wide range of movement).
Child doesn't respond even to strong stimulation.
Associated problems such as poor vision, hearing, speech and difficulty in feeding.

If the child has such low tone that he can hardly hold himself up against gravity, it will be easy to recognise the features described. But if his tone is not so very low, you will need to recognise the same features when they are less obvious.

Figure 3.9

Child with low tone.

Figure 3.10

Child with very low tone: Needs a lot of support.

Child can't use hands to play because he needs them to support his trunk. It is important to know that in a very young child, features of flaccidity are often only temporarily present. As the child tries to become more active, the tone changes, and you may find transitory spasticity or fluctuating tone that shows itself briefly before the child becomes flaccid again.

Mixed tone

Children with athetosis and ataxia often also have spasticity. This may mask the involuntary movements and tremor, but these will be seen if the spasticity is changed.

Athetoid and ataxic children are often flaccid when they are young. The features of athetosis and ataxia show themselves only when the child attempts to move.

This is a brief picture of each of the different kinds of CP. If it is possible for you to match the picture you have built up of the child you are assessing, to one of these descriptions, then you can record your classification. Sometimes it is not easy to decide straight away.

Figure 3.11

Mixed (athetosis with spasticity): This young man uses spasticity in his upper limbs to give him fixation.

Figure 3.12

Child shows low tone in trunk but fluctuating tone in arms.

Section 2

This section describes how to record all the other information about the child under the report headings suggested earlier. Family concerns are a key part of the assessment and should be recorded, but the issue of working with families needs a whole chapter and will not be described here (see Chapter 6).

History

Under this heading, you record what you know from the medical records of the child's birth history and any following events that are relevant. This is a good place to also record any other impairments the child may have. These associated problems could include,

- Visual impairments
- Hearing impairments
- Learning problems
- Epilepsy
- Perceptual problems
- Speech problems
- Feeding problems

It may not be possible for you to know all the additional problems the child may or may not have at the first or second meeting, but at least you should record those that you do know.

General impression

Under this heading, you give a brief picture of what the child is like as a person as opposed to a 'case'. Is she friendly or frightened, interested or unresponsive, dependent on her mother or eager to explore? Try to give, first of all, the positive things about the child so that someone else, looking at your report, will be given the positive as well as the negative aspects of the child's condition.

There are some general personality characteristics that go with the different kinds of CP that might be useful for you to know, but of course, each child is an individual and it would be a mistake for you to think that, for example, every athetoid child has the same personality.

Athetoid children in general, can show abrupt changes of mood, almost echoing their changes in postural tone. Although their constant movement makes it seem as if they have poor concentration, in reality they can show surprising persistence and determination and this helps them to achieve a good deal. It is important for you to remember that most athetoid children have normal intelligence, and this too helps them to achieve.

The child with spasticity, in contrast, can be fearful of moving and of being moved. This leads him to dislike changes and to be unadventurous and rather passive. Some children with spasticity, however, love to be moved as long as they feel secure with the person handling them.

Abilities

It is good to have on the first page of your assessment a clear list of things the child *can* do, and briefly, *how* they do it.

No matter how disabled a child is, he will be able to do something. Maybe he can just turn his head or take weight on his legs when placed in standing. Maybe he can indicate his needs by showing movement with his hands. As long as what he does can be said to have a useful function, it is an ability, even if he uses abnormal patterns to achieve it.

In this list you should include not only those abilities that you have seen for yourself, but also those the parent tells you about. For example, a child may not be ready to show you that he can crawl, but his mother may say that he crawls everywhere at home. You must record in the notes what his mother describes and try later to see for yourself.

The list of abilities should state briefly *how* the child functions. (e.g., can crawl but uses too much flexion.)

Inabilities

These are the functional activities that he cannot do and which you and the family will be working towards achieving. You must think of,

- What postures he cannot maintain
- What handling and movement he cannot tolerate
- What hand function he has not got
- What mobility around his environment he has not got
- What sequences of movement he cannot achieve

For an older child with severe spasticity and fixed contractures, you will not mention that he cannot walk alone. You might instead say that he cannot sit alone and that he cannot tolerate being placed in standing because sitting alone and tolerating being in standing are what your aims of treatment will be. Walking alone would be very ambitious for such a child.

Basic tone

Here you record your findings of the child's tone at rest and how it changes as he is moved or tries to move.

Postural patterns

This term is used to describe the combination of activity in different muscle groups as the child holds himself in different postures and as he moves. Under this heading, you record the child's posture and movement in each of the positions in which you assessed him, and as he moved from one to the other. For example, you might say, 'In supine, he holds his head turned mostly to the right, his shoulder girdle is retracted, his elbows are flexed and pronated (left more than right) and his hands are fisted.' It is a good idea to record if, in general, the child is showing a pattern that is more flexed than extended, and if one side of the body is more affected than the other.

A normal child of one year or more will show an endless variety of movements. Patterns of flexion and extension will be broken up and mixed together so as to be unrecognisable. It is this integration of flexion and extension that leads to the development of rotation (from 6 months onwards) that is so important for balance and coordination.

A child with spasticity, on the other hand, will show a limited variety of movements. He uses patterns that are coordinated, but they are not efficient or good for function because they are stereotyped or always the same. For example, if a child with spasticity tries to reach and grasp, he may be able to extend his elbow, but because he moves in an abnormal stereotyped pattern, this extension causes his hand to open and his forearm to pronate. He cannot, therefore, grasp an object and turn it over to look at it.

Figure 3.13

Grasping leads to flexion of whole limb. With normal grasp there is extension of the wrist.

The patterns that children with spasticity use to move and function are sometimes called total patterns. This means that if a child starts to use one element of a pattern, then the whole pattern is likely to follow. For example, if he grasps a toy with his hand, this is likely to cause his whole arm to move in the flexion pattern. Again, if he is placed in long sitting, his extended knees may cause his feet to plantarflex (extensor pattern), his hips to adduct and inwardly rotate, making it difficult for him to bring his trunk forward over his pelvis because the extensor pattern makes him push backwards.

Figure 3.14

Passive extension of the knees in this position causes the hips to extend as well.

The diagram on the facing page shows the mixture of patterns that can be seen in the movements of children with spasticity. For example, the upper limbs can show flexion pattern at the same time as the lower limbs show extension; or maybe the right side will show flexion pattern and the left extension.

You may see a child using the flexion pattern in his upper limbs in combination with extension in his lower limbs. For example, in a child with spasticity in long sitting, you will see that his legs are in the extension pattern but his head may be flexed and so also his arms and upper trunk. You may also see a child using the flexion pattern in one position and the extension pattern in another. For example, a child with spasticity lying prone may show a pattern of flexion—with her head down and unable to lift it up,

Abnormal patterns of coordination associated with hypertonus

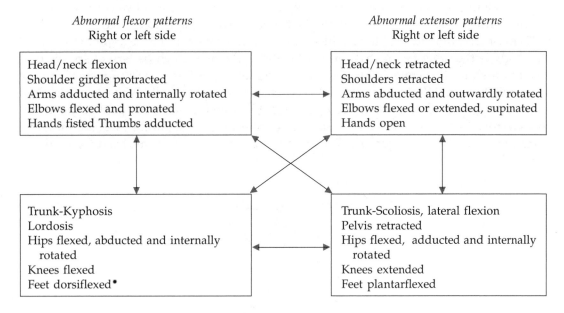

Abnormal flexor patterns Right or left side	*Abnormal extensor patterns* Right or left side
Head/neck flexion Shoulder girdle protracted Arms adducted and internally rotated Elbows flexed and pronated Hands fisted Thumbs adducted	Head/neck retracted Shoulders retracted Arms abducted and outwardly rotated Elbows flexed or extended, supinated Hands open

Trunk-Kyphosis
Lordosis
Hips flexed, abducted and internally
  rotated
Knees flexed
Feet dorsiflexed*
	Trunk-Scoliosis, lateral flexion
	Pelvis retracted
	Hips flexed, adducted and internally
	  rotated
	Knees extended
	Feet plantarflexed

shoulders protracted, elbows flexed, hips abducted and outwardly rotated, and knees flexed because of the influence of gravity. The same child, when held in standing, may go up on her toes, adduct and internally rotate her hips and extend her knees (extension pattern).

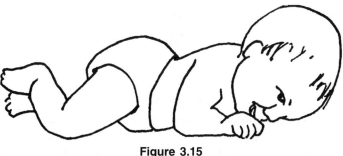

Figure 3.15

Gravity pulls child into total flexion pattern.

These changes have causes. Very often, a child with spasticity will be flexed in prone and extended in supine because of the influence of gravity. This reaction is present in a normal baby in his early weeks. It makes him flex more when the anterior* surface of his body is stimulated by contact with the supporting surface, and extend more when he is on his back and it is the posterior* surface of his body that is being stimulated. Normal babies lose this reaction as they become more able to come up against gravity. Children with moderate spasticity lose it to some extent, though they may always remain under its influence. Children with severe spasticity may never be able to be free of it.

In most children with CP, the position of the head in space and in relation to the rest of the body is the other factor that can predictably influence which pattern of spasticity is seen in a child. If a child is moving only in abnormal patterns, any movement of the head will have an effect on the rest of the body. For example, a child who sits on the floor with a good deal of flexion may be in danger, when he lifts his head, of shooting over backwards. A child who can only weight-bear on his legs in standing by going into total extension, may be in danger of collapsing into flexion if he flexes his head forward.

Figure 3.16

Legs are in extension pattern while arms are in flexion.

Another reaction that is related to the head and is modified in normal babies, is often seen in children with CP. This is the Asymmetrical Tonic Neck Reflex (ATNR). The ATNR is seen when a child's head is retracted and turned to face in one direction: the arm and leg on the opposite side flex, and those on the same side extend. This is sometimes known as the 'bow and arrow' posture because it is the posture used for shooting an arrow from a bow. Children who have this reaction have great difficulty keeping their heads in midline. They also find it hard to bring two hands together in front of their eyes, or to bear weight on two straight arms.

In your recording, the important thing is for you to get a clear picture of the patterns the child is using most, either to hold herself up against gravity or to move and function.

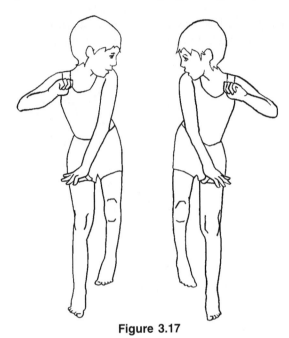

Figure 3.17

ATNR causes flexion pattern in right arm with head turned to left
and flexion pattern in left arm with head turned to right.

In particular, you will want to know which patterns she is using at home every day when she is placed in different positions, or when she moves about.

As you record the child's postural patterns, it is also important to record any asymmetry. A child who is able to use one part of her body better than others is in danger of **associated reactions**. This means that the more effort she puts into using the part of her body that functions better, the greater the spasticity becomes on the more affected side. Associated reactions can also be seen when a child uses her arms to compensate for lack of movement in her legs, and the spasticity in her legs increases as a result. A child with spastic diplegia who uses a lot of effort to walk with crutches will have increased spasticity in her legs. Also, a child with hemiplegia who uses the unaffected side to function and neglects the affected side, will have more spasticity as a result of associated reactions.

You may have noticed that children who can move about on the floor or can walk a little, do so in an abnormal way. Children with spasticity in their legs find it difficult to take steps and very often, if they are crawling, find it quicker to move both legs forward at the same time. This is called bunny hopping because it resembles the way rabbits hop. Children who learn to walk must obviously be able to take steps, but you will have noticed that these steps are small and the movement abnormal.

Both these ways of moving are caused by **lack of dissociation** between the legs. This is a result of the child using total patterns of movement. If one leg flexes, the other tends also to flex. If the leg extends, so also does the other. The child who learns to walk despite these difficulties (usually a diplegia or a moderate quadriplegia) has to use a great deal of compensation by moving his trunk to make up for the lack of movement in his legs.

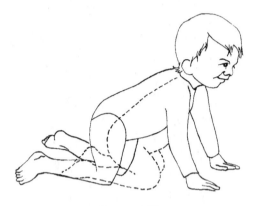

Figure 3.18

Total pattern of flexion in legs leads to lack of dissociation and bunny hopping.

Contractures and deformities

A contracture is tightening in muscles or joints that cannot be stretched out without surgery. It is caused by a group of muscles pulling more powerfully than its antagonist group over a long period of time. That is to say, the overuse of one abnormal pattern.

When you first see a child, you will need to check all his joints and the muscles likely to be contracted, to see if he has already developed these. You must also know how to anticipate which muscles and joints are likely to develop contractures. This subject will be looked at in detail in Chapter 4.

A deformity is an abnormal position of a part of the body. It involves bones, joints or soft tissues. It can be fixed or unfixed. That is, it can be corrected passively or it cannot. You will need to note any fixed or unfixed deformities you find in the child you are assessing. There will be more information about this in the next chapter.

Section 3

Main underlying problems

The main underlying problems refer to the reasons why a child is unable to achieve basic motor functions. As you picture the child you are assessing, you will need to identify 2 or 3 functional activities that at present he cannot do but which you think it might be possible for him to achieve with help. It is particularly important to take into account what he himself would like to be able to do, and what his family would like him to be able to do. Now, looking back at your report describing his tone, his patterns of movement, and his attitude to learning new activities, you may be able to understand the causes of his problems.

You may find a picture of repeated abnormal patterns of movement that are at the root of the problem, or you may find more of a picture of lack of basic stability or involuntary movements interfering with the child's ability to function. Here are two very different examples.

- The mother of a 2-year-old child with severe spastic quadriplegia who is very irritable and doesn't make eye contact or smile, is having great difficulty handling him for daily care activities because he pushes back into extension with any kind of stimulation.

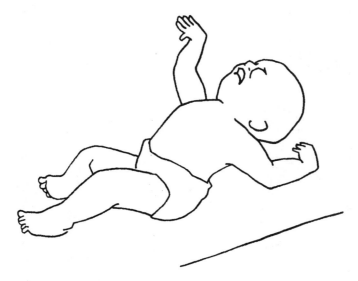

Figure 3.19

In supine: Head, shoulder girdle and arms extended, legs like new-born.

The therapist, in her assessment, found that the child in supine turned his head always to one side and pushed vigorously back into extension with his shoulders retracted and abducted, and his elbows flexed (extension pattern). His legs were somewhat flexed and abducted (primitive). In prone, however, he could not lift his head, which was turned to one side, his back was rounded, his shoulders protracted and flexed, and his hips also flexed (flexion pattern). Held in sitting, he was mostly flexed until he tried to life his head—then his whole body pushed back into extension.

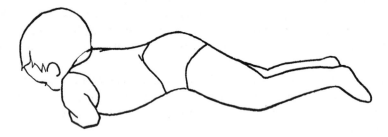

Figure 3.20

In prone: Flexion pattern.

Figure 3.21

In sitting with head flexed, arms in flexion pattern.

Figure 3.22

In sitting with head raised, arms in extension pattern.

In her report under the heading of Main Problems, the therapist wrote that the child's spasticity was such that he could only move in total patterns that were abnormal. These patterns depended on his position, and any movement, stimulus during handling, or position of his head, influenced the rest of his body. He could only move in response to these abnormal reactions and, therefore, could not function in a normal way.

- A young athetoid child was struggling to learn to roll over from supine to prone, but every time she got to prone, her arm would become trapped underneath her body. If she lifted her head, she also turned it, and this made her flip back into supine. This was making her unhappy to be in the prone position, and instead of learning to roll over, she was beginning to push herself backwards across the floor in supine.

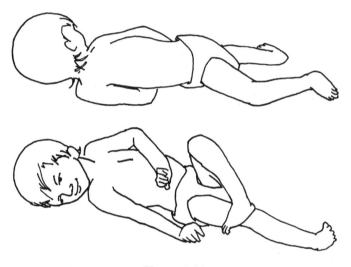

Figure 3.23

Athetoid girl rolls half into prone. Arm gets stuck under her body, and as she lifts her head to try to free it, her head turns and she flips back into supine.

The therapist worked out that the reason for her arm becoming stuck was that in prone her head was more flexed. The position of her head influenced the rest of her body. In this case, her flexed head prevented trunk extension and didn't allow her to lift her body up enough off the floor to free her arm.

I hope these examples and those in the following table will help you to understand the possible underlying causes of the problems that children with CP have. By analysing and naming them, you will be more able to focus your efforts as well as those of the child and his family on achieving useful function. It is important to realise though, that these are just examples and each child is different.

Some possible main problems interfering with a child's motor functions

Inability	Possible causes				
	In severely spastic	*In moderately spastic*	*In athetoid*	*In ataxic*	*In child with low tone*
To maintain head and trunk erect when placed in sitting or standing	• Predominating pattern of flexion or extension	• Competition of patterns (abnormal pattern of flexion combined with abnormal pattern of extension)	• ATNR—asymmetry • Lack of co-contraction • Involuntary movements • Poor proximal fixation • Fluctuating tone, especially with effort	• Lack of sustained co-contraction • Poor proximal fixation • Unreliable balance reactions	• Poor co-contraction • Tone too low to lift trunk and head against gravity • Pulled into gravity
To bring hands together in supine	• Extensor pattern predominating due to influence of gravity	• Asymmetry • Extension pattern predominating due to influence of gravity	• Asymmetrical position • Poor co-contraction, preventing holding of position • Involuntary movements	• Poor proximal fixation • Lack of sustained co-contraction	• Insufficient tone to lift arms forward against gravity • Poor proximal fixation • Lack of sustained co-contraction
To tolerate lying prone when placed	• Influence of gravity increases flexor spasticity and prevents active extension • Fear of not being able to lift head increases spasticity	• Flexion pattern likely to predominate • Intermittent flexor spasms may cause discomfort	• Active extension against gravity is not good enough to lift head • Intermittent flexor spasms may cause discomfort	• Poor proximal fixation • Lack of active extension leading to fear or frustration and dislike of position	• Inadequate active extension against gravity • Fear and dislike of position

(continued)

(*continued*)

Inability	Possible causes				
	In severely spastic	*In moderately spastic*	*In athetoid*	*In ataxic*	*In child with low tone*
To balance in sitting when placed	• Exaggerated co-contraction	• Predomin-ance of flexion or extension • Unable to break up abnormal patterns	• Involuntary movements • Poor proximal fixation • Lack of co-contraction of head and trunk • No support of arms	• Lack of sustained co-contraction • Poor proximal fixation • Inadequate balance reactions	• Tone too low to hold body up against gravity • Poor co-contraction
To come to sitting from supine	• Exaggerated co-contraction	• Unable to break up patterns— with head flexed, can't extend arm and take weight on it	• Inadequate flexion of head and trunk against gravity • Poor proximal fixation	• Poor proximal fixation • Tendency to use total patterns— therefore, no rotation	• Lack of flexion against gravity • Poor co-contraction and difficulty in mobile weight-bearing on extended arm
			• Difficulty in weight-bearing on arm	• Poor co-contraction and difficulty in mobile weight-bearing on extended arm	
To take steps in crawling or in standing	• Exaggerated co-contraction • Use of total patterns • No rotation	• Use of total patterns leading to poor dis-sociation between legs • No rotation	• Lack of co-contraction • Poor grading of movement • Poor proximal fixation • No balance • No rotation	• Poor balance reactions • Poor proximal fixation • Poor grading of movement • No rotation	• Poor co-contraction • Lack of extension against gravity • No rotation

4

Contractures and deformities

A contracture is a permanent shortening of a muscle, muscle tendon or joint structure. Once a contracture becomes established, fibrous tissue is laid down, and it can then be lengthened only by surgery.

A deformity is an abnormal body posture or limb position. Holding this abnormal position prevents the whole range of normal movements from taking place and the abnormal position becomes more fixed. The joints and muscles involved become less flexible and permanent changes take place in them. Even the bones can change their shape. The deformity is then said to be fixed.

A growing child who cannot hold normal postures or move in normal ways is in great danger of developing contractures and deformities. This is because of the unequal pull of one group of muscles (usually a result of the dominance of the flexor pattern) on the child's pliable bones and joint structures.

As therapists, it is one of our main responsibilities to anticipate which contractures and deformities a child is in danger of developing, and then to do everything possible to prevent it. There is only a short time in a child's life to do this. If we fail, the child will become a young adult who will be difficult to look after and who would have lost what possibilities he might have had to do things independently. Besides all this, he may be in pain because of his joints being out of alignment or even dislocated, and there will also be the distress of a disfigured appearance. All in all, it is worthwhile to work hard to prevent these secondary effects of CP.

Testing for contractures

When you test a child's range of joint movements to see if he has contractures, it is very important to make sure that he is relaxed, comfortable and not in any way anxious about what you are doing. You will need to ask his mother to talk or sing to him or tell him a story so that his attention is not on what you are doing.

As you stretch out his muscles, hold his limbs supported in a comfortable way and make sure that your hands stay in contact with him. When there is spasticity and you feel strong resistance, maintain your pressure until the spasticity gives a little. At the same time, be careful not to increase the spasticity by fighting against it and causing fear and pain.

In the lower limb, the groups of muscles in which contractures most commonly occur are,

> *the calf muscles,*
> *the hamstrings,*
> *the hip flexors*, particularly psoas major,
> *the hip adductors*, and
> *the hip inward rotators.*

The action of the calf muscles is to plantarflex the foot and flex the knee. Therefore, to stretch these muscles, the knee needs to be extended and the foot dorsiflexed. A normal range is 45 degrees of dorsiflexion beyond 90 degrees. The child should be comfortable in a semi-lying position with his legs in some abduction and outward rotation, so that the hamstrings are not put on a stretch.

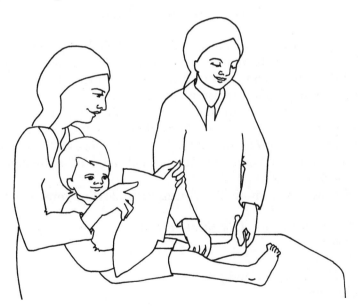

Figure 4.1

Testing for contracture in the calf muscles.

The action of the hamstrings is to extend the hip and flex the knee. If there is a contracture, it will be difficult to straighten the knee with the hip flexed. To test for hamstring contractures, have the child in side-lying with the under leg semi-flexed at the hip and knee. Test the upper leg by first flexing the hip to a right angle and then straightening the knee. If the knee cannot be straightened fully, extend the hip a little and then test again.

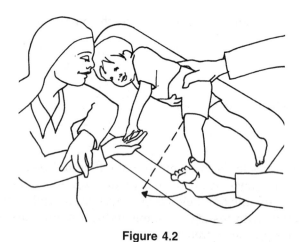

Figure 4.2

Testing for hamstring contracture.

To test for hip flexor contracture, have the child in side-lying with the under leg fully flexed to fix the pelvis. Test the range of extension in the hip of the upper leg, making sure that it is neither abducted nor adducted, and neither inwardly nor outwardly rotated. Normally, there is 15 degrees of extension past the midline.

To test for contracture of the adductors, have the child lying supine and test the range of abduction in both legs. Try first with the knees flexed and then with the knees extended. At the same time, test for contractures of the inward rotators with the knees both flexed and extended (see Figures 4.3 and 4.4). The normal range of abduction with extended hips is 50 degrees–80 degrees.

Upper limb contractures commonly occur in the following muscle groups:

adductors and internal rotators of the shoulder joint,
flexors of the elbow,
pronators of the elbow,
flexors of the wrist and fingers, **and**
adductors of the thumb.

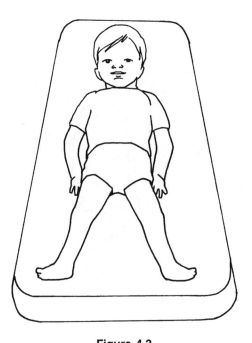

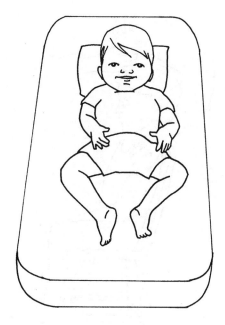

Figure 4.3

Normal limit of abduction and outward rotation with knees straight.

Figure 4.4

Normal limit of abduction and outward rotation with knees bent.

These muscle groups can be tested with the child in sitting or supine. The adductors and internal rotators are tested by elevating the arm in abduction and outward rotation. The other groups are tested by carrying out the opposite movement to the action of the muscles (see Figures 4.5 and 4.6).

In older, more severely affected children, contractures of the wrist flexors occur because they are propped in sitting so that the flexion pattern predominates in the upper trunk and arms, and because they have had no opportunities to bear weight on outstretched arms.

Children who do not move much, either because of spasticity or hypotonicity, will in time develop limited range of movement in their joints, which may become permanently altered. A child with severe spasticity will have exaggerated co-contraction and both flexor and extensor groups of muscles will be shortened. The child will then be limited to a small range of movement in the mid-position.

The child with marked hypotonicity may often be left in supine with his legs pulled by gravity into abduction and outward rotation (frog position). In time, his abductors and outward rotators may become shortened, and it may be difficult to extend, adduct and inwardly rotate his hips.

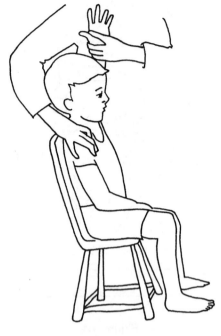

Figure 4.5

Testing range of movement in shoulder,
elbow, wrist and hands.

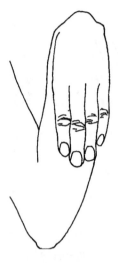

Figure 4.6

Contracture of wrist flexors, elbow pronators
and thumb adductors.

Deformities

The bony changes and joint subluxations and dislocations that occur most frequently in
children with CP are as follows:

- Claw toes
- Rocker bottom feet
- Patella displacement
- Hyperextension of the knee
- Hip subluxation
- Hip dislocation
- Lordosis
- Kyphosis
- Scoliosis
- Upper limb deformities such as shoulder dislocation, elbow dislocation, and ulnar
  deviation of the wrist and thumb

Claw toes

Toes that are held in flexion can become fixed in a kind of claw position. This is either because of predominantly flexor spasticity or to compensate for poor coordination of the leg and trunk muscles in the child's efforts to balance. Eventually, it will not be possible to fully straighten out the toes, and the child will have less possibility of having a good base for standing. The toes may also be difficult to fit into shoes.

Figure 4.7

Claw toes deformity.

If you notice a child is standing with his toes held mostly in flexion, you can prevent claw toes becoming a fixed deformity by placing a small lift under his toes inside his shoe, and by using felt or sponge to hold his toes in abduction (see Figures 4.8 and 4.9).

Rocker bottom feet

This deformity gives the child's foot the appearance of the rocker bottom of a rocking chair. It is caused by the child's difficulty in getting his heel to the ground because he is using the spastic pattern of extension (which includes plantarflexion at his ankle) to hold himself up against gravity. The arch of his foot flattens to compensate. Later, the weight of his body habitually pressing down on the arch reverses its curve. By the time he reaches adulthood, the changes in the joints and ligaments of his feet will cause him pain (see Figures 4.10, 4.11 and 4.12).

To prevent rocker bottom feet, you must first reduce the spasticity in the child's hips and pelvis, and give him better active extension against gravity. Some weight-bearing every day with his feet and legs in a good position and the possibility of active extension in his hips will help. You must teach him how to stretch his own tendo-achilles in weigh-bearing. You also need to make sure that all children who cannot actively lift up the long arch of their feet are given shoes with arch supports.

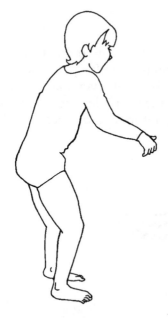

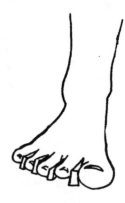

Figure 4.8

This girl is flexing her toes to compensate for poor control of hips and knees.

Figure 4.9

Separating toes with sponge wedges may prevent claw toes.

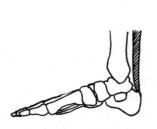

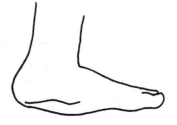

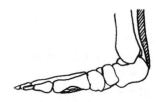

Figure 4.10

Bony arch of a normal foot.

Figure 4.11

Rocker bottom foot deformity.

Figure 4.12

Bone position in rocker bottom foot.

Splints

This book cannot cover this subject in much depth. Where there are resources and good orthotic expertise, there will be a wide choice of splinting available, especially for children who walk up on their toes. Where there is some orthotic expertise and where light plastic material is available, it is worthwhile making ankle foot orthoses (AFOs) for these children. The aim is for the AFO to hold the heel in alignment (not allowing it to swing medially or laterally) and to prevent plantarflexion of the foot during walking. The child wears the AFO inside her boot or shoe, and will need a larger size than normal to accommodate it. It must be a very good fit, and it is the therapist's responsibility to see that it does not cause pressure sores.

It is important to remember that if the AFO holds the foot in dorsiflexion, this is likely to increase the child's tendency to flex the hip and knee. Therefore, while wearing AFOs, a child must be encouraged to actively extend her hip and knees.

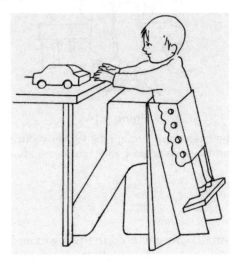

Figure 4.13

Spending time in a forward tilting standing frame with arch supports or ankle foot orthoses prevents rocker bottom foot deformity and encourages active extension of hips and knees.

Footwear

Medical boots are often heavy and may look unattractive. If they are not achieving a useful purpose for a child, try to avoid them. A child whose ankle joint inverts* or everts* when weight-bearing may be helped by a well-fitting boot. If a boot has a narrow enough heel that grips the calcaneous,* it can also help to prevent plantarflexion*. However, not many boots fit the child in this way. Well-fitting shoes with an arch support are probably the most advisable footwear for the majority of children.

When putting on shoes, have the child in sitting on a stool with his knee flexed to a right angle and his foot on the floor. Make sure the shoe is wide open. If you can, slip your finger under his toes to make sure they are not flexed. If this is impossible, push down on the child's knee while feeling through the shoe to see if his toes are flexed. When you are sure the toes are straight, fasten the shoe.

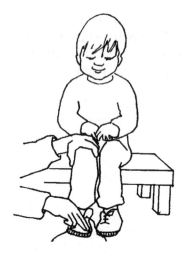

Figure 4.14

Pressure on the knee down through the leg will reduce the spasticity
in the toes. Fasten the shoe only when you are sure the toes are straight.

Patella displacement

The patella (kneecap) is a small bone enclosed in the lower end of the quadriceps muscle.
If there is an unequal pull on either the medial* or lateral* heads of quadriceps, the
patella will be displaced and will not be able to function as an efficient lever for
straightening the knee.

Children who are able to walk alone but with slightly flexed knees (crouch gait), very
often develop pain in their knees. This is caused by the patella being drawn upwards,
away from its usual connection to the femur. It can even result in the child being unable
to continue walking (see Figure 4.15).

Hyperextension of the knee

This happens when the structures at the back of the knee joint become lax and allow the
knee to overextend. It is often seen in a child with low tone who compensates for
inadequate hip extension by locking her knees in extension (see Figure 4.16).

However, it can also be seen in a child with tight tendo-achilles, who can get his heel to
the ground only when walking by hyperextending the knee.

A third, uncommon reason for hyperextension of the knee arises if the hamstring
tendons have been overreleased during surgery.

Figure 4.15

Crouch gait describes the way a child walks when his knees and hips are always slightly bent.

Figure 4.16

This child has poor active hip extension. She compensates with hyperextension of her knees and lordosis (hollowing of the lower back).

Subluxation of the hip

In all new-born babies, the acetabulum is shallow and insubstantial. It becomes more able to hold the head of the femur only if the baby moves his legs against the pelvis in kicking and later takes weight on his legs either in crawling or standing. It is the movement of the weighted head of the femur that deepens and shapes the bony cup that will hold it in place. A child who does not have the opportunity to stand and move may, therefore, be in danger of having an inadequately formed acetabulum, and the head of his femur may slip in and out. When he is young this may not cause any problems or discomfort, but he is sure to have pain as he gets older, especially if the head of the femur is pulled out of its place by spasms.

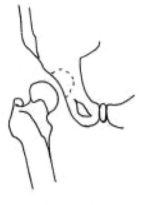

Figure 4.17

In a normal baby, during the first year, the head of the femur deepens the cup of the acetabulum.

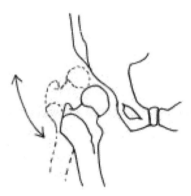

Figure 4.18

Without full range of abduction and outward rotation, the acetabulum is shallow and the head is not held in place.

Hip dislocation

This is more serious than subluxation. When the hip is dislocated, the head of the femur stays outside the acetabulum. It may be displaced either anteriorly or posteriorly. If it is anteriorly dislocated, it sits below and medial to the anterior superior iliac spine. If it is posteriorly dislocated, it sits above and behind the acetabulum. Posterior dislocation is more common and is mostly seen in children who flex, adduct and inwardly rotate their hips with spasticity in order to function. A child who is in danger of this will be one who rarely takes weight on her legs, and who lies in supine with windswept* hips. The hip that is more adducted and inwardly rotated is in most danger. Anterior dislocation is mostly seen in children who spend a good deal of their time lying supine with their legs in a frog position (hips abducted, flexed and outwardly rotated).

To test for a posteriorly dislocated hip, place the child in supine and make sure that his pelvis is level. Flex both of his legs so that his feet are on the floor and his legs together. If he has a dislocated hip, the affected leg will appear to be much shorter. If the hip is anteriorly dislocated, you will be able to feel the head of the femur in the child's groin. If it is posteriorly dislocated, the greater trochanter will be more prominent on the affected side and it will be higher and more posterior than on the unaffected side.

Figure 4.19

The right hip is dislocated. Because the head of the femur is outside the acetabulum, the right thigh seems much shorter than the left.

A child who has a dislocated hip is very difficult to place in a normal comfortable sitting position. This is because it is difficult for the hip to be flexed to a right angle. As the child gets older, she may also suffer pain and discomfort in the joint.

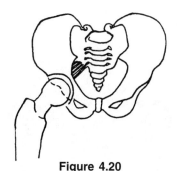

Figure 4.20

Head of femur in normal position in deep acetabulum.

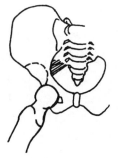

Figure 4.21

Head of femur dislocated anteriorly.

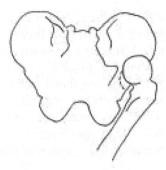

Figure 4.22

Back view of pelvis showing head of femur dislocated posteriorly.

Lordosis

A child who cannot actively extend her hips when placed in standing is likely to hyperextend her knees and extend her lumbar spine to compensate. This causes a lordosis deformity which can become fixed if the child has to use this pattern a lot to walk about.

Figure 4.23

Lordosis or hollowing of the lower back develops either in compensation for kyphosis or as a means to bring the trunk upright when active hip extension is not adequate.

Kyphosis

A child may develop a kyphosis to compensate for a lordosis, or he may develop a kyphosis as a result of flexor spasticity of the trunk. A child with spasticity who is placed in prone will try to lift his head, but because the flexion pattern always predominates in prone and because of the effect of using effort, his flexor spasticity will increase. This will make it impossible for him to actively extend his head and trunk.

Children who can't sit up alone are often propped in sitting in the corner of a chair or sofa. If they are placed with a straight trunk and hips flexed at right angles, it is most likely that they will flop forwards or be pulled forward by flexor spasticity and may even fall on to the floor. For this reason, most mothers leave their children with their hips in some extension and their trunks leaning backwards, supported by a cushion. But in this position, if the child tries to come forward to reach with his hands, he will only be able to flex from his upper trunk and shoulders. This is because of the mainly extensor pattern in his legs. He may be able to use his hands a little in this way, but all the time the spasticity will be increasing in his trunk, putting him in danger of a fixed kyphosis.

Figure 4.24

Flexion in the upper limbs and trunk to compensate for too much extension in lower limbs causes kyphosis in a child with spastic quadriplegia.

Scoliosis

Scoliosis occurs when there is a pull down in the muscles of the trunk that is greater on one side than the other. The children who are found to have the worst scolioses are those with fluctuating tone. A child with fluctuating tone usually has great difficulty holding her trunk and head erect. So, for safety, her mother is likely to leave her lying in supine on the floor. In this position, the child can maybe learn to roll on to her side, but she is likely to be able to roll more easily to one side than the other. In time, the pull down in the favoured side of her trunk will cause a fixed scoliosis.

Once a child has a fixed scoliosis, it is even more difficult for her to actively extend her trunk. It is also very difficult to place her in a good sitting position. Meanwhile, the scoliosis becomes more and more pronounced until the child's breathing becomes restricted and she becomes prone to chest infections.

Less severe scolioses are seen in children with hemiplegia, diplegia or moderate quadriplegia. In these cases, the scoliosis will be caused by the imbalance of muscle pull in the trunk or by shortening of one leg because the child does not take as much weight on that side as on the other. All scolioses, including the less severe, will lead to back pain and loss of movement of the spine later in life.

Upper limb deformities

Although these can cause discomfort and reduction of function, they are not so threatening as they involve the trunk and lower limbs. It is beyond the scope of this book to describe them in detail. But as in all deformities, they are caused by unequal pull in uncoordinated muscles, and can be prevented by good positioning and the child's own activity in more normal postures and patterns of movement.

Can surgery help to correct contractures and deformities?

Surgery should be done only if all else fails to elongate tight muscles. It is better to do it when the child is over 8 years old, so that it will not need to be done again as he grows.

All surgery does damage and leaves muscles weaker than before. But it is preferable to pain caused by subluxated or dislocated joints. If there is X-ray evidence that the head of the femur is increasingly less covered by the acetabulum, release of the adductor muscles and ilio-psoas can reduce the risk of dislocation. This is not likely in children who walk alone. It is more likely in children who walk with aids and most likely in those who don't walk at all. Children with spastic quadriplegia who sit with windswept hips, are in danger of having one hip dislocate posteriorly and the other anteriorly. Research has shown that in these cases, both hips should be operated on at the same time to avoid dislocation switching to the opposite hip. Without surgery, the hip will become painful and it will be difficult to find good seating for the child.

If tendo-achilles need lengthening, this should not be done before the child is 8 years old. After surgery, the plaster cast should hold the ankle at 0 degree dorsiflexion, not

5 degrees or 10 degrees. The child should not wear the cast for more than 2 to 4 weeks. She should walk as soon as the cast is dry.

In all cases of surgery for children with CP, there must be good communication between the surgeon, the therapist and the family so that the reasons for surgery are well understood by the family, and so that the therapist can follow the surgeon's plan for the child responsibly.

5

Principles of treatment

The most important thing to know and understand about treating children with CP is that each child needs his own programme and no one child is the same as another. It is not possible to say 'This child has diplegia, therefore, this set of exercises is what he needs.' This is because one child with diplegia will function in a different way from any other. Also, the way to make changes to one child's abnormal tone and postural patterns to meet his needs and deal with his problems may be different from the way that might work with another child. The same is true for all the different kinds of CP. That is what makes treating these children such a challenge.

In order to meet this challenge, we are going to consider the principles governing the range of treatment techniques that we can use to increase and improve the child's functional abilities and prevent contractures and deformities. In a later chapter, we will be looking at how treatment can be adapted to fit the circumstances that the child and his family find themselves in.

Before you can do that though, you have to know what treatment may be effective and how you can carry it out. In order to be effective, your treatment programme should,

- *Prepare the child for function at her appropriate level*. By level, I mean what is appropriate for her developmental stage and her needs. Treatment should prepare her to achieve a specific goal that will give a better quality of life for her and her family, but one that is within her developmental stage and intellect.
- *Incorporate in the treatment the child's own activity*. Enable her to be active either in holding a position or moving. Help her to start an interesting or challenging activity; then withdraw support so she carries on alone.
- *Make tone more normal to make coordination possible*. By handling and guiding the activities, we can reduce the spasticity in a child with raised tone, increase tone in a child who is hypotonic, and steady the tone in a child who is athetoid or ataxic.
- *Give the child sensory experience of more normal movement*. Helping the child to move and play with better coordination will give him the feeling of what is normal. The more often he can carry out that more normal movement the more it will be laid down in his central nervous system, and the easier it will become for him.

How do we make tone more normal?

When a child has spasticity or athetosis, he moves in abnormal patterns which are not functional. We can facilitate the child to function better while counteracting any abnormal tone by the use of positioning, weight-bearing, handling and movement.

Positioning a child in supine, as we have seen in our assessment, increases extensor tone. In prone, the flexor tone* is increased. We can use this knowledge in treatment. For example, we would not treat a child with strong flexor spasms in prone on the floor unless we could reduce those spasms in some way. Similarly, it would be very difficult to treat a child who pushes back into extension in supine on the floor.

In treatment, we position the child in ways that **break up the abnormal patterns**. We do this by changing one, or maybe two, elements of the abnormal pattern and substituting a part of a different pattern. These broken-up patterns are called **tone influencing patterns (TIPs)**. For example, imagine a child with moderate quadriplegia placed in cross-legged sitting on the floor. His head will be pulled down, his shoulders protracted and his arms flexed and pronated. He cannot balance much, nor can he reach forward for a toy or even lift his head to look around him.

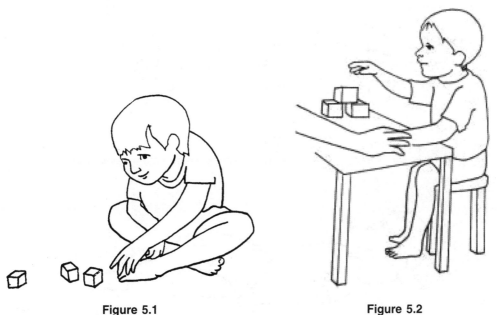

Figure 5.1

Child in cross-legged sitting. Too much flexion prevents him from reaching out with his hands.

Figure 5.2

When he sits up on a chair, the pattern is broken (his legs are not abducted and outwardly rotated), so he can reach better.

If, however, we take away one or two elements of the flexion pattern (abduction and outward rotation of his legs) and place him in sitting on a stool, provided he can extend his trunk, he will be able to balance and use his hands better. This is because his legs are now less flexed, less outwardly rotated and more adducted. The flexion pattern is broken up.

Another example is of a child who pushes back into extension in supine. Her head is extended and turned to one side, her legs are adducted, extended and inwardly rotated, and her mother has great difficulty abducting her legs in order to change her nappy. If she flexed her head forward by placing it on a small pillow, this might be enough to break up her pattern of extension, and her legs would more easily flex and abduct.

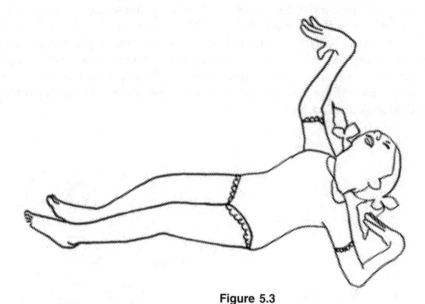

Figure 5.3

For this girl, when she lies on her back, the extension pattern takes over.

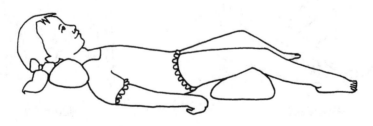

Figure 5.4

The extension pattern is broken up when her head and knees are flexed.

When we put a child in a position, we have to also consider the subject of **mobile weight-bearing**. Positioning a child in such a way that he is helped to bear weight through his limbs or trunk, and at the same time he moves (or is moved) a little, will reduce spasticity and prepare him to maintain functional postures. For example, a child who has some flexor spasticity and finds it difficult to lift his head when placed in prone, may be helped by being placed on a mobile surface such as a roll. This position also gives him the possibility of taking some weight through his extended arms, which further reduces the pull down in his shoulders.

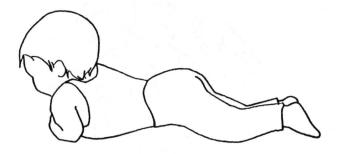

Figure 5.5

Arms flexed under body increase flexor spasticity.

Figure 5.6

Mobile weight-bearing on arms reduces spasticity.

A child with athetosis or ataxia placed in standing, bearing weight through an extended arm on a table in front, will have more possibility of symmetry and coordinated co-contraction because the weight-bearing, as he moves and plays, regulates his tone and controls overshooting.

Figure 5.7

Mobile weight-bearing on legs regulates the tone of a child with athetosis.

We have seen that by using positions, we can not only reduce a child's spasticity but also facilitate more normal postures and movements. The key to further facilitation is through **handling**. The way we touch and move the child will have a very powerful effect, so we must make sure that this effect is good. It helps to know that just through one point at any one time, we can control, change and guide postures, tone and patterns of movement in other parts of the child's body. These points are called **key points of control**. They are the points where we place our hands in order to stimulate the child, as well as to reduce his spasticity and facilitate normal postures and movements. Key points can be **proximal** or **distal**. Proximal key points facilitate more activity distally. Distal key points work only if the child has some postural control proximity.

Figure 5.8

Child with diplegia uses better arms to pull to stand. This increases extensor spasticity in legs.

Figure 5.9

Therapist reduces spasticity, stimulates activity and facilitates extension and weight-bearing through key point.

In the case of a child with spastic diplegia, the therapist would be using a **proximal key point** if she placed her hands on the child's upper legs while in standing. With her hands in this position, she can use her thumbs to facilitate extension, and her fingers to turn the child's hips into outward rotation. Her hands can also tip the child's body weight forward to get good alignment in the lower limbs, pelvis and trunk. The effect would be to reduce the spasticity in the lower limbs and facilitate hip extension and weight-bearing through feet with heels flat on the floor.

An example of a **distal key point** would be in a child with hemiplegia where the therapist uses the child's hand, in particular, the base of the thumb on the hemiplegic side, to change the abnormal pattern of movement in the whole arm. At the same time, she can shift the child's weight over on to the hemiplegic leg. This will only be effective if the child has good enough proximal activity to allow him to accommodate to the stimulation.

Figure 5.10

In a child with hemiplegia, the therapist uses distal key point of control
(base of thumb) to outwardly rotate, extend and supinate the arm,
at the same time facilitating weight-bearing on affected leg.

The most commonly used **proximal** key points of control are the **head, spine, sternum,***
shoulder girdle and **pelvis/hips**. The most commonly used **distal** key points of control
are the jaw, wrists, knees, fingers, jaw, base of thumbs, ankles and big toes. But **how** do
we use the key points of control? What should we do with our hands when they are
placed on the chosen key point of control?

It is not easy to describe this in writing. There is no substitute for demonstration and
practical training, but a few guidelines are possible. These are:

- Keep your hands firmly on the child. A light, moving touch is too stimulating and
  cannot be used to control or guide. But equally, a tight grip will not be comfortable
  or effective. Your hands must feel all the time what is happening in the child's
  body.
- Keep clearly in your mind the elements of the posture or movement you are working
  for. Keep using the key point of control in such a way that the child becomes active.
  Remember, the child is learning a whole new posture or movement by feeling it
  happen in his body. If he starts to be able to do for himself the activity you are

helping him with, you will feel him become light to your touch. You can then withdraw your support until he needs it again.

- Move the child to reduce spasticity. Fairly slow movements in a small range in the trunk, shoulder girdle and pelvis will reduce spasticity proximally. Once the tone in the proximal parts is reduced, you must use key points for wide ranges of movement in the limbs and trunk.
- Use your hands to support the child in positions that will be useful for him while stimulating him to be active in other parts of his body.

We have looked in general at the principles of treatment. Let us now look at how we can apply these principles to each of the different kinds of CP in turn. But at this point, I must issue a warning. The examples I have given as treatment in each type of CP *must not* be looked at as 'recipes' for treatment of that condition. The examples are necessary to illustrate a way of putting a principle into practice, but you should not think that each example is the one and only way to treat that particular type of CP.

Principles of treatment in severe spasticity

- **Analyse the predominant pattern of spasticity that is interfering with function.**
- **Use patterns which prepare for functions with wide ranges of movement.**
- **Avoid functional activities which increase flexion, e.g., crawling, kneeling, W-sitting.**
- **Work for righting equilibrium* and saving reactions to decrease fear.**

Through your assessment, you will have found out which pattern of spasticity is predominant. In the child with severe spasticity this may be flexion or extension, or the child may be almost rigid when both flexion and extension are equally present. In the **predominantly flexed** child, you will see a fairly symmetrical position but there is likely to be more side flexion in one side of the trunk than the other, and the pelvis will be retracted on that side. If you remember, in children with severe spasticity, the tone is higher proximally than distally, so your first objective is to reduce the tone in the trunk, pelvis and shoulder girdle and then work in the pattern that will prepare the child for function. In the case of the flexed child, the danger of contractures is great even while very young. You must, therefore, use every position and situation you can think of to get the child extended. Use gravity to help you, and once you have got the child in an extended position, use key points to facilitate him to actively extend and abduct his limbs in wide ranges of movement and to bear weight through the limbs and trunk.

There is no avoiding the fact that all this takes time. But if you can find the most effective way to help the mother make her child with severe spasticity looser and easier to handle, she will agree that is time well spent.

Possible positions in which to treat a flexed child with severe spasticity

1) **Supine, head down on mother's legs** (if the child is small enough). In this position, gravity facilitates extension, and if the mother moves her legs a little, it will help to reduce the spasticity.

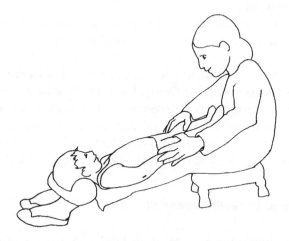

Figure 5.11

Mother moves her own legs one after the other to reduce the
spasticity in the child's trunk. Gravity facilitates extension.

2) **Side-lying on mother's knee on side that is more flexed.** If that side is elongated before the child is put in position, the weight-bearing will reduce the spasticity. In this position, the child can be facilitated to reach out with his upper arm and to kick into extension and abduction with his upper leg. Later, he can perhaps be facilitated to roll into prone and lift his head and trunk.

3) **Carrying in side-lying position.** As the child is lifted and moved from place to place at home, this way of carrying can be good treatment. The more flexed side is kept elongated and the mother's arm between the child's legs keeps them abducted, outwardly rotated and extended. Holding the child like this but more into prone will facilitate him to lift his head and trunk against gravity as long as the flexor spasticity can be reduced (see Figure 5.12).

From these starting positions, the child can be moved carefully into any other position that you feel will give him the best possibility of holding an independent posture or carrying out some activity that satisfies him.

Predominantly extended children are very difficult for mothers to handle. They push backwards with their heads and sometimes their whole bodies against the mother's arm when she is trying to hold or carry them. They do this in response to a whole range of

Figure 5.12

Carrying position for strongly flexed child.

stimuli whether pleasant or unpleasant, and the mother has aching arms and a feeling of being rejected by her child. The first priority in our treatment is to make it easier for the mother to handle her child. She needs to be given a way of carrying him so that he doesn't push into extension.

Figure 5.13

Difficulty in controlling a child with severe extensor spasticity.

One way could be to have the mother tuck him under her arm, holding his legs in flexion, abduction and outward rotation. In this position, his head will have nothing to push against and the mother's arm around his shoulders will keep them in protraction.

This, combined with holding his hips in flexion, should break up the pattern of total extension.

Figure 5.14

Possible alternative carrying position.

Feeding can be extremely difficult too. This is because, as the child pushes back into extension, his mouth opens and his tongue pushes forward. A good position that changes this is to have the child sitting between his mother's knees, while she sits on the floor. The child's hips and knees are a little flexed. His mother keeps his shoulders forward and also presses her hand against his sternum. This is a good key point from which to reduce neck retraction.

Figure 5.15

Severe extensor thrust makes seating and feeding difficult.

Figure 5.16

Alternative position for feeding or play.

There is a danger though, that children with severe spasticity who have patterns of total extension, will suddenly change to a flexion pattern.

It is, therefore, important for you to begin working as soon as possible for active extension of the head and trunk against gravity, and also extension, abduction and outward rotation of the limbs. A good way to do this is to have the child in prone across your knees. Slight movement of your knees will reduce flexor spasticity. Use the shoulder girdle or pelvis as a key point of control to rotate the trunk and facilitate the child to lift his head, thereby getting active extension in his whole trunk. You can later use your forearm on the trunk to maintain the extension while your hands are free to facilitate abduction and extension of the limbs.

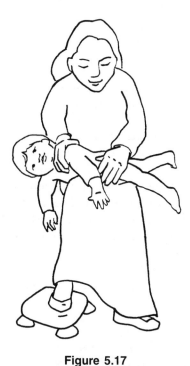

Figure 5.17

Reducing spasticity in the trunk using rotation.

Figure 5.18

Using forearm to maintain extension leaving hands free.

Another big problem with extended children is that they are in great danger of hip dislocation because of the spastic pattern of adduction and internal rotation of their legs. This pattern also makes it difficult for the mother to change the child's nappy. These two problems can be alleviated at the same time if the mother can use the time during nappy-changing to reduce the pattern of spasticity.

She can do this by having the child lying supine with the head flexed forward on a small folded towel. She may also need something under each shoulder to protract the shoulder girdle. It should be possible to bring the child's hands down to her sides at least momentarily. Once she has adjusted to the position, the mother can start working on her legs, but she should keep talking to her so that she learns to enjoy the position.

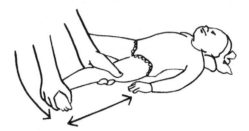

Figure 5.19

Step 1: Bringing the first leg into outward rotation and abduction, and then pushing the whole leg upwards into the acetabulum.

To begin with, the mother tips the child's pelvis forwards and backwards a little to mobilise it. Then she works on one leg to bring it into as much outward rotation, extension and abduction in the hip as she can with the knee in extension and, if possible, the foot in dorsiflexion. She pushes upwards through the leg to push the head of the femur into the acetabulum (see Figure 5.19). This action also reduces the spasticity. She then keeps the leg in this position with her forearm while she does the same thing with the other leg (Figure 5.20). Finally, she rests both forearms on the child's thighs to hold the whole position, and uses her hands to lift the child's pelvis. At the same time, she can ask the child to help her lift her bottom (Figure 5.21). All this will not happen in just the right way the first time it is tried. It may take weeks, but it will become easier each day.

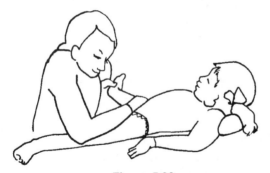

Figure 5.20

Step 2: Holding the first leg in position with forearm while bringing the second leg into abduction and outward rotation.

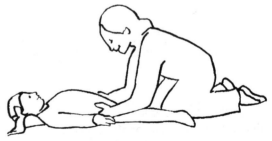

Figure 5.21

Step 3: Keeping both legs in position with forearms, mother helps child to actively lift her bottom off the floor.

This exercise to reduce spasticity and facilitate active extension with abduction of the hips is good preparation for placing the child in standing. The child should be lifted into a standing position without allowing any flexion to happen in the hips or knees. You will see the child finding it easier to actively extend her hips and knees now, than she would have done with no preparation.

Figure 5.22

Step 1: Roll child on to side and lift her without flexing hips or knees. Hold her close to your body.

Figure 5.23

Step 2: Keep holding her in extension as you bring her into a standing position.

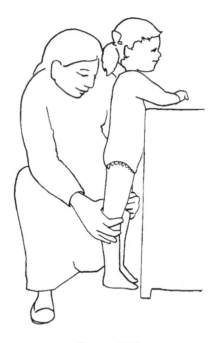

Figure 5.24

Step 3: Place her in standing, still keeping her in extension.

Principles of treatment in moderate spasticity

- Reduce tone by countering the patterns of spasticity and by avoiding too much stimulation and effort.
- Avoid using stereotyped patterns of movement for function, find ways to break them up.
- Facilitate sequences of movement.
- Facilitate wide ranges of movement in tone influencing patterns (TIPs).

The main problem that children with moderate spasticity have is the danger that as they grow and become more challenged to achieve independence, they will use their abnormal patterns of movement to function and their spasticity will increase. The reason the spasticity increases is because they are using more and more effort. The more effort they use, the more **associated reactions** they will acquire. Associated reactions occur if they use the more able parts of their bodies to compensate for the lack of a choice of patterns in the more affected parts.

In a young child, we have the opportunity to prevent the worst of this effect. This is not to say that we can make the child normal, but we can prevent the escalating build-up of spasticity and the neglect of the affected parts. This, in turn, will help to prevent contractures and deformities.

Knowing how the child functions at home or at school is very important. A child with moderate spasticity who spends a good deal of his time crawling with very flexed legs will have difficulty learning to walk. This child must have a walking aid that supports him in a standing position and allow him to take some weight on his legs in a correct position and move around independently. This will prepare him for walking, whereas crawling is more likely to prevent it.

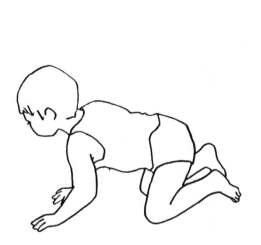

Figure 5.25

Crawling, using too much flexion.

Figure 5.26

Taking weight on feet and pushing on the ground facilitates extension, and is a better way for the child to move around.

Whatever abnormal pattern we see the child using, we must work to counteract. This should be done not just in treatment, but much more importantly, in everyday life as well. The young child with hemiplegia who learns to bottom shuffle in side-sitting, retracting his affected side behind him, must be facilitated to take weight on his affected side in sitting, standing and in sequences of movement. He must also have opportunities to take weight on his affected arm and outstretched hand while he plays. This will not only facilitate better function, it will also help to prevent associated reactions brought about by his efforts to play using just his unaffected hand.

Mobile weight-bearing is the key to a child being able to change from one position to another. Children with moderate spasticity need help to take weight on limbs with abnormally high tone. Once they can be placed with weight through the limb, however, the trunk can be moved (by the mother or therapist) against the limb. This not only reduces the spasticity, it is also a very good sensori-motor experience for the child. This is preparation for sequences of movement.

Figure 5.27

Therapist facilitates child to take weight on her right arm. He uses abduction and outward rotation of left arm to reduce spasticity, and from this point rotates the trunk against the weight-bearing arm.

Figure 5.28

It is then quite easy to place her weight-bearing through two outstretched arms. He can later take her back to side-sitting so that she gets the experience of changing her position from side-sitting to crawling and back.

Some children with moderate spasticity experience **flexor spasms** in their hips. These are uncomfortable, even painful, and children soon learn to be apprehensive about being placed in the positions that they know can cause them spasms. Fear increases the possibility of spasms occurring, so it will be necessary for you to make sure that a child's treatment is at all times interesting and satisfying for him. The spasms are less likely to happen if you are able to prepare the child first by reducing the flexor spasticity at the hips. You can do this with the child in prone by pressing down on his sacrum and rocking him a little from side to side to rotate the spine. Those children who have spasms when lying prone on the floor will be easier to treat across their mother's knees or over a large roll or ball. This is because they will be lying on a mobile surface, and the movement reduces the spasticity.

Figure 5.29

Therapist holds legs in extension, presses down on child's sacrum and moves the child slightly backwards and forwards on the roll. This reduces the flexor spasms and facilitates extension in his head and trunk.

Figure 5.30

It should then be easier to bring him to standing. To reduce the flexor spasms, the therapist keeps pressure on the sacrum and gives some pressure down through the child's legs. He holds the child's arms forward to prevent any pull down.

The following table gives more ideas about how to use key points of control.

Use of key points of control

Key point and tone influencing pattern (TIP)	Likely effect
Child prone, head and neck extended, shoulder girdle retracted	Facilitates extension in rest of the body
Child supine, head and neck flexed, shoulder girdle protracted	Reduces extensor spasticity
Inward rotation of shoulder with protraction of shoulder girdle	Reduces extensor spasticity and is useful in athetoids if used carefully. But in children with spasticity, it increases flexor spasticity of neck, trunk and lower limbs
Outward rotation of shoulder with supination and elbow extension	Reduces flexion and increases extension in the rest of the body
Horizontal abduction of arms in outward rotation with supination and elbow extension	Reduces flexor spasticity. Facilitates opening of hand. Facilitates abduction of the legs with outward rotation and extension if spine is also extended
Extension of arms backwards in prone, sitting or standing with spine extended	Reduces flexor spasticity. Has same effect as in horizontal abduction but is easier to achieve when there is more spasticity
In sitting, prone or standing, abduction of thumb with arm in outward rotation and supination	Facilitates opening of fingers
Outward rotation of legs in extension	Facilitates abduction of hips and dorsiflexion of ankles

Principles of treatment in athetosis

- Stabilising of posture through controlled stimulation and small range of movement.
- Weight-bearing and compression to facilitate co-contraction and reduce involuntary movements.
- Work for symmetry and midline orientation.
- Facilitation of head and trunk control and proximal fixation to give child a chance to control distal movements.
- Use of placing and holding to facilitate sustained tone and better grading of movement.
- Facilitation of arm reach and grasp.

The movements of children with **athetosis** are jerky and quick and in wide ranges. They lack stability, symmetry and grading of movement. In particular, they lack head and trunk control when they try to hold themselves up against gravity.

Without treatment, a child with athetosis is likely to be left in supine on the floor because there he is safe from falling. Propped in sitting, his extensor spasms are likely to put him in danger of falling backwards and hitting his head. It is very likely that he will hate being put in prone because the poor stability in his trunk will make it difficult for him to lift his head, use his hands or move about. What usually happens is he learns to push himself about in supine on the floor using his abnormal extension and good legs, while his arms push back uselessly in extension, outward rotation and retraction beside his head on the floor. This situation needs to be prevented if he is to develop any head any trunk control or any hand function. In fact, the first essential in treating children with athetosis is to get them up off the floor and put them in weight-bearing positions against gravity.

Figure 5.31

Pushing backwards along the floor is an easy way for an athetoid child to move about, but it prevents him from using his hands or developing head control.

Figure 5.32

Giving him opportunities to take weight on both arms and legs counteract the child's desire to push himself around in supine.

Weight-bearing and compression through the child's limbs or trunk while in alignment will increase the tone and facilitate the child to hold a posture. The more opportunities he gets to hold useful postures, the better able he will be to control the involuntary movements himself. While he is learning to do this at first, however, he will not be able to tolerate much stimulation. The child with athetosis needs to build up tolerance to stimulation. During treatment or while he is practising at home, he needs people to talk quietly to him so that he can begin to keep still in standing or sitting with weight-bearing and whatever support is necessary. His attention at this time should be focused on listening to a family member telling him a story or showing him pictures in a book. The book, or the person talking, must always be presented in the midline position so that the child does not turn his head and become asymmetric. As soon as possible, he can then start using one hand with help to manipulate a toy.

Figure 5.33

Therapist facilitates child to take weight on right arm while building tower with other hand.

Figure 5.34

Once the child is able to take weight on his elbows, he may be able to drink from a 2-handled cup by himself.

As he learns to hold positions, the child must also learn to move, but without moving in wide ranges. If, for example, he becomes able to keep his head in midline and take weight through his arms in a supported sitting position, he could be facilitated to grasp a cup with both hands and bring it to his mouth. Or, perhaps he becomes able to be supported in standing so that he takes weight equally well on both feet. Most children with athetosis take weight well on one leg while the other flexes and extends in a way that does not allow weight-bearing or even functional stepping. Once he can bear weight equally well, he can be facilitated to take steps. This should be done in such a way that his body is in alignment and his head in midline. Many athetoid children use their ATNR to take steps. They turn their heads to the right to get extension and, therefore, weight-bearing on the right leg, and then they turn their heads to the left when they want to switch weight to the left. It is very difficult for the child to take steps in a more normal way once he has learnt to use this reflex action. Using the ATNR like this also prevents him from being able to keep his head in midline and look where he is going.

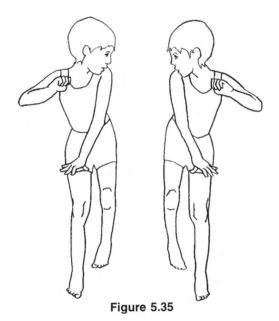

Figure 5.35

Child using head-turning to take steps. This reinforces his asymmetry.

Children with athetosis, even more than other children, love to be on their feet and to be helped to take steps. This may be because their legs are often less affected than their arms, and as long as someone else holds and controls their trunk and arms, they know how to take steps. As treatment, helping a child with athetosis to walk is only useful if the child is kept in alignment and is facilitated to take his full weight through his legs. Most families will help their child to walk by having him lean back against them while his legs take dancing steps way ahead of his body. This is not useful. The pictures on the following pages show some ways in which a good pattern of walking can be given. There are many other ways depending on how the child's involuntary movements need to be controlled and how much support he needs in his trunk.

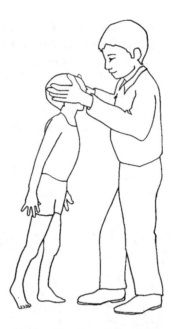

Figure 5.36

By holding the child's head in midline, the therapist can keep him
symmetrical and keep his body weight forward over his feet.

Figure 5.37

The therapist is preventing involuntary movements in the child's arms
at the same time as keeping her body weight forward and
giving pressure down through her legs.

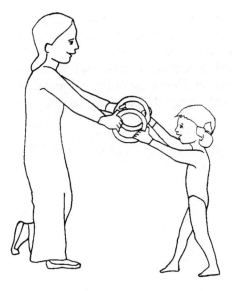

Figure 5.38

Holding on to the rings in this way keeps the child symmetrical and
allows the therapist to give more or less support as needed.

Figure 5.39

Holding the child's arms forward in extension gives symmetry
and therapist can keep the child's body weight forward.

Enabling the child to **reach and grasp** is another essential part of the treatment of an athetoid. For many children, just having both hands grasping a piece of broom handle while keeping their heads in midline is a huge task. In order to learn to tolerate it, they must be placed in a position that is symmetrical, and does not allow them to throw themselves back into extension. Held in standing is probably the best position, but sitting in a chair with the hips kept firmly flexed is also good.

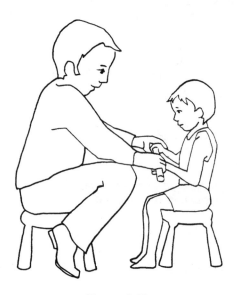

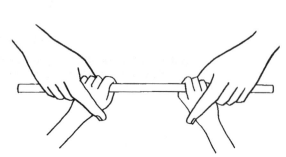

Figure 5.40

Having his head in midline and both hands held on the stick can be difficult for an athetoid child to tolerate.

Figure 5.41

Detail showing how therapist uses forefinger to hold child's wrist in extension while maintaining grasp.

The broomstick is then placed in the child's hands and the therapist facilitates bilateral grasp with wrist extension and both arms in forward extension. Once he has learnt to tolerate this, the therapist can move the stick in various directions to give the child the sensori-motor experience of grasping in different directions. The grasp can also be changed between pronation and supination. All the time, the therapist is talking to the child so that there is eye contact and midline orientation. As always with facilitation, the therapist uses her hands sensitively, assisting the child only as much as necessary, so that he learns to control his own movements.

Figure 5.42

Once child can tolerate both hands grasping with straight elbows,
he will be more ready to reach and grasp.

Although children with athetosis have strong extension in supine and in sitting when they often throw themselves backwards uncontrollably, this extension is not useful for function. In order to acquire good trunk control, they need **active extension against gravity**. Prone would be the best position in which to acquire this, but most children with athetosis strongly object to being placed in prone. It may help such a child to be placed across her mother's knees and have the mother raise one leg up on a low stool so that the child is not horizontal. Gravity, in this position, will not have such a strong influence and the child can be facilitated to raise her head and trunk and hold them in extension for a few seconds. As she becomes more able to hold the extension against gravity, the mother can reduce the angle to make the child more horizontal. This is a good position in which to dress and undress the child.

Figure 5.43

Using prone position over mother's knees for dressing and undressing helps the child to learn to tolerate being in prone and getting active extension of his head and trunk.

In order to facilitate better **proximal fixation**, the therapist must use her hands on the child's pelvis, shoulder girdle or trunk to hold these proximal parts steady and in alignment, and enable the child to have the experience of using his hands or legs in a useful way. Without this facilitation, the only way the child can fix himself proximally is to hold his trunk, shoulder girdle or pelvis in extreme positions, using his head to initiate the movement into the position. Since a child with athetosis almost always has his head turned to one side or the other and never in midline, the rest of his body will also be asymmetrical. Treatment must, therefore, give him the experience of holding his shoulder girdle midway between protraction and retraction, of keeping his trunk midway between flexion and extension and no side-bending or rotating to either side. The pelvis also must be kept in alignment and not retracted or hitched up to either side. If all these parts are aligned, the child will be more likely to be able to maintain postures against gravity in preparation for learning fine motor skills.

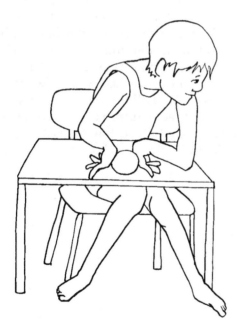

Figure 5.44

An athetoid child with poor trunk control tries to fix himself using his arms and legs.

Figure 5.45

With his pelvis fixed by knee blocks and his trunk supported by a table he can more easily keep his head in midline and use his hands.

Principles of treatment in ataxia

- Control postural tone by weight-bearing and joint compression.
- Place and hold child in positions to facilitate co-contraction. Encourage child to take over so that you can release hold.
- Use mobile weight-bearing and graded movements to change from one position to another.
- Get selectivity of movement and independence of limbs from trunk.
- Work for rotation around body axis.
- Facilitate balance and protective reactions.

A child with **ataxia** may be falling over a lot or having great difficulty in steadying himself and coordinating his movements in order to dress himself or hold a spoon to feed himself. Your assessment of the child with ataxia will show where he is failing in carrying out motor functions.

He falls over because the postural tone in his trunk and pelvis is inadequate, and also because he lacks grading of movement. He can't hold a spoon because his shoulder girdle does not hold his arm steady, and maybe also because he has intention tremors or overshoots.

To help him not to fall so much, the child needs the sensorimotor experience of recovering his balance when gravity threatens him. You will need to put him in positions where he is vulnerable, but where he can be facilitated to accommodate to the threat of overbalancing. For example, hold one of his legs off the ground as he stands and ask him to reach with each arm in turn in all directions. Don't let him fall, but don't support him so much that he is not stimulated enough to respond to prevent himself falling.

Figure 5.46

Facilitating balance reactions.

Make him weight-bear on both arms while you lift his legs (wheelbarrow walking). If his tone is very low, you will need to support him above his knees. Get him to take steps so that he has to actively extend against gravity and rotate around his body axis (see Figure 5.47).

Dressing and undressing himself should be a very important part of the child's treatment. Find the best position for him to use all the activities of dressing—sit to stand, raise one leg, raise both arms overhead—so that he is having treatment at the same time as learning to be independent.

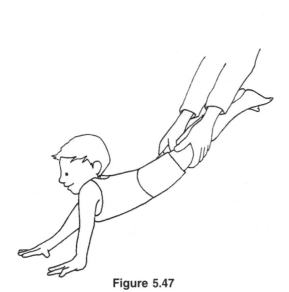

Figure 5.47

Wheelbarrow walking is a good way to facilitate proximal (in this case trunk and shoulder girdle) control.

Figure 5.48

Learning to walk with long poles with a broad base gives a child with ataxia confidence. The therapist can give as much or as little support as is necessary for the child not to fall.

Children with hypotonia

It is rare for a child to continue to have very low tone. Usually they change, sometimes quite quickly, to being athetoid, ataxic or spastic. If they do continue to have low tone, they are likely to also have problems with seizures and learning difficulties. In this case, the main aim of treatment is to make them as active as possible and to find good positions in which they can be managed, and those that will not cause contractures and deformities.

In young children who have low tone, you must be careful when stimulating them so that spasms don't suddenly take over. There is also a great danger of a child being placed in positions that would be appropriate for low tone, but if flexor spasticity starts to appear, he could quickly develop contractures.

Principles of treatment in hypotonia

- Work for sustained co-contraction.
- Have the child work against gravity.
- Use weight-bearing through all the limbs and in all positions.
- Use sensory stimulation and joint compression.
- Use vocalisation and laughter to build up tone.
- Treat slowly—give child time to respond. Sustain positions to give child sensori-motor experience.
- Be aware that low tone in young children can change to abnormally high tone or fluctuating tone.

The following pictures show a mother using joint compression and exciting stimulation to help build up enough tone to help her daughter hold her head and trunk erect. After jumping the child up and down with her body in alignment, she places her in standing and uses her whole hands to tap downwards through her shoulders. If the child can hold the position very briefly, the mother can lift her hands off momentarily before tapping again.

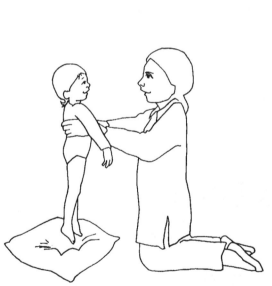

Figure 5.49

Bouncing on soft surface with child's head, trunk and legs in alignment facilitates co-contraction.

Figure 5.50

Tapping through the child's shoulders with her body in alignment also facilitates co-contraction and helps her to hold herself upright for a short time.

Children with mixed CP

The guiding principle in treating children with mixed CP is that you should treat what you find. In particular, look for how each child tries to compensate. For example, children with athetosis, who continue to have poor postural control in their trunk, as time goes on, very often develop flexor spasticity in their legs because they use their legs to give themselves fixation. Children with ataxia sometimes show spasticity when they start to stand. They may stand with adduction and internal rotation of the hips to give themselves stability, but they will lack active hip extension.

Figure 5.51

Ataxic child showing some spasticity in standing.

Figure 5.52

Prepare her to stand better by facilitating active extension in her whole body.

If a child is hypotonic, stimulate him enough to give him some ability to hold himself up against gravity. If he shows signs of involuntary movements, make sure you work for head and trunk control, and symmetry and midline orientation. If he shows signs of spasticity, use key points of control and TIPs to facilitate more normal patterns that will lead to independent functional activities.

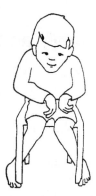

Figure 5.53

Athetoid boy trying to give himself fixation by hooking his feet around the chair legs.
This will increase the tone in his legs and may lead to flexor contractures.
Treatment should aim to give him better trunk control.

Final word on treatment

This chapter has, I hope, given you an idea of the principles on which a treatment programme can be based. The examples given may or may not work for the child you are treating. They are only examples. In each child you treat, you will have to work out the most important thing to achieve, and make sure your treatment is aimed at achieving that. If it does not work, change your treatment, but stick to the principles.

6

Therapist, family and child working as a team

This chapter will be looking at ways in which therapists and families can best relate to each other and work together.

I have chosen to talk about families rather than parents because very often the entire extended family can work in partnership with the therapist to help the child function better at home. Although in most cases mothers are the main carers, sometimes a brother or sister has more time than a mother to use play to help the child to function better. Sometimes an aunt or uncle can persuade a child to do more difficult activities. This is not a criticism of the mother; it is more a realisation that a mother's relationship with her child may not always be compatible with her working with him as a therapist does. A child looks to his mother for protection and comfort. Exercises may challenge him and make him feel insecure, and he may feel confused if it is his mother who instigates such a feeling.

Another reason for choosing to work with the wider family is that the attitude of the family as a whole can have a huge impact on how the mother feels about her child, and even how she handles him in his daily care. This makes it important for therapists to seek opportunities to work with other members of the family as well as the mother.

This chapter is divided into two parts. Part 1 deals with the issue of partnership between therapist and families. Part 2 deals with how therapy can be carried out as part of daily care.

Section 1

How therapists can be good partners

Research has shown that, no matter how expert the treatment, physiotherapy or occupational therapy alone cannot make a significant improvement in the child's condition. There has to be carry-over from the treatment into the child's everyday life.

As therapists, it is our responsibility not only to help families understand this, but also to enable them to do it.

This poses a problem for many therapists. Instead of treating a child themselves and using their skills to enable him to do things he could not do before, they are being asked to pass on their hard-earned knowledge and skills to every family, no matter what its circumstances or education may be. Many therapists feel a threat to their professional status in this.

I think we should look at it like this: as therapists we have knowledge and skills that enable us to assess and design a programme for children of all ages and with all types of CP. We are passing on to each family the understanding and skill that they need to enable them to work with their own unique child. By doing this, we are planting the seeds that allow an effective partnership to grow and develop. Besides this, there is the even more compelling reason that if we don't teach the families what we know about their children, we cannot bring about any lasting improvement in their condition.

So, as well as being therapists, we must also be teachers and trainers. To some extent, we have to also be social workers because before we can work with a family, we have to understand a good deal about them. We need to know,

> what their *attitude to the child and his disability* is,
> what their *home situation* is like,
> what *coping mechanisms* they have,
> what *capacity for learning* they have, and
> what *relevant knowledge, skills and insight* they have.

We have to learn the skills that will enable us to gather this information from the family without seeming to be just curious. This requires that we develop a friendly way of behaving and interacting with them. At the same time, they have to feel able to trust us to keep the information that they give us totally confidential. They have to feel safe that the secrets they share with us will not be used for anything except for the benefit of their child.

I think there are very few therapists who have been trained to do these things as part of their basic education. They are expected to learn them 'on the job', often without any role models. This is a very difficult thing to do. It means making a fundamental change in how you see yourself as a therapist. In order to do this, it might help to look at some recent material that has been written about the role of professional people.

Reading the research, as a professional, can be depressing. Professional people, it seems, are not very popular! This attitude to professionals is reflected in the findings of a number of research projects that showed that patients and clients felt oppressed by the power they felt that professionals exerted over them.

In his book, *Challenging the professions*, Robert Chambers describes how rural communities in developing countries were the last people to be consulted after economists and engineers had planned a project. After the project had been completed, it was discovered that it was quite inappropriate for local needs. If only the professionals had consulted local people in time, a lot of money and effort would have been saved. Situations like this have encouraged people planning services to feel they can manage without professionals. In some countries, community-based rehabilitation programmes are being run without therapists because the planners say that therapists bias the programme towards the *medical model* when what local communities want is the *social model*.

The medical model tends to focus on the individual as a patient, attempting to make him or her as 'normal' as possible. Control of rehabilitation is solely in the hands of medical experts. Success or failure is seen only in terms of how the medical programme enables the disabled person to conform to what society regards as normal. Those who cannot achieve this 'normality' are considered failures by society, and of course, the therapists will also feel they have failed.

The social model tends to imagine that impairment is not the real obstacle. Efforts are focused on encouraging the community to accept the person just as he or she is, and on adapting structures within the community to accommodate disabled people's needs. Control of these efforts is much more in the hands of the community and of disabled people (or their families) themselves.

The balanced model is the model accepted by the World Health Organisation. It combines and integrates good quality individual rehabilitation with efforts to bring about social inclusion for the child and his or her family. In this model, the evaluation of needs and the search for solutions are shared between all concerned in a cooperative way.

I have seen the failure of the medical model in many of the countries where I have taught. In these countries, I have often heard therapists make complaints about parents. 'They don't care enough about their children to work with them', 'They are not educated enough to understand the importance of treatment' or 'Parents are lazy, they just want us to do all the work.'

I believe what happens is this: Parents come to the therapists with the hope and expectation of a medical cure for their child's condition. They are likely to be very worried and depressed about their child and they are not likely to be impressed by a cure that comes in the form of exercises that may seem just like playing. And so, either they do not comply, or they carry out the exercises but without any faith in their value. After some time, they lose hope that even these efforts can make any difference.

The therapist, on the other hand, has a huge number of children to treat. It is tempting to concentrate time and effort on those families who listen easily to advice, who understand that the exercise programme will help, and who have enough time and energy to give to their children. The therapist thinks, 'It's not my fault if people don't listen to my advice,' and he or she takes less and less time and trouble over those families who seem not to care. In the end, they stop coming and the child is left untreated at home. In places where there are only a few therapists and a large number of children to treat, this happens to the majority of children. Only a few parents are able to act on the therapist's advice.

The social model may be successful in giving the family and the child a much better environment in which to function. Families, however, will very often worry that their child is not having opportunities to learn to walk, for instance. This is because no one involved with the programme has the necessary expertise to advise them as to how they can best help with this. Without good therapy, it is also certain the dangers of contractures and deformities will be much greater.

Padmani Mendis in her paper on CBR wrote that when physiotherapists (or well-trained rehabilitation workers) were involved in a programme, the output, both in terms of quality and coverage, was greater. So, there is recognition that expertise is necessary.

It is not, however, the existence or not of the expertise that is in question, it is the way in which this expertise is delivered to people with disabilities or their families, that can be a problem. In his book, *Disability, Liberation and Development*, Peter Coleridge has written in a very sensitive and telling way about the relationship between therapists and people with disabilities. He says, 'nobody is arguing for fewer professionals: let us be very clear about that. They are vital. What is at issue is the underlying attitude they bring to the job. What disabled people want is to join with professionals in formulating policy on rehabilitation and then to work with them to implement it. This is an exciting positive process which in no way detracts from or undermines the importance of the professional task; on the contrary, it enhances it.'

The 'underlying attitude' he is talking about is the way in which therapists tend to think of the people they work with—as 'cases' or 'patients' rather than people. A 'case' is something to be cured and made 'normal'. What disabled people (and this includes children and their families) want, is to be seen as a whole person. To do this the therapist needs to,

- include them in the planning of the child's programme,
- help the family and child to accept what cannot be cured, and
- always work towards functional goals that the child or family have chosen, and that help towards social integration.

We must give up the idea that in some way, we are in control of the children and their families. We are there to serve their needs, and we can only do this by understanding those needs and by using our knowledge and expertise to help the family to meet them in their own way.

One of the most important tasks we have is helping the family to come to terms with their child's condition. Both therapists and parents have the difficult task of realising that therapy can give good but limited results. Through therapy, some children will become independent, maybe become able to earn a living; others will become partially independent, and still others will only become easier to look after. This can be a painful and difficult realisation. The process of acceptance will be slow and costly, but without it there will only be disappointment and despair.

There are personal qualities that we can develop in the same way that we develop handling skills, that will help us in this difficult task. These qualities are being able to,

- *listen and show you understand,*
- *allow the family to participate as equal partners,*
- *give information clearly,* and
- *teach handling skills.*

Listening and understanding

These skills need to be thought about the practised. Not being listened to is one of the most frequent complaints families have against some professionals.

We need first to think about what makes for good listening. Think about the following list of elements of good listening and ask yourself how many of them you employ in your listening to families.

- **Put aside your own opinion.** Don't judge parents, and don't allow your own assumptions to interfere with your ability to pay attention and absorb information from them.
- **Keep an open posture.** Does the way you are sitting show that you are interested? Sitting with crossed legs and folded arms, for example, can make you look tense and impatient. Your posture should show that you are relaxed but attentive.
- **Eye contact.** The amount of eye contact you make will vary from one culture to another. The important thing is to make sure that you make eye contact in the right way to give the parent the feeling that you are taking in what he or she is saying.
- **Facial expression.** Again, this will vary from one culture to another. But the way you change your facial expression as you listen, should reflect your interest and sympathy. It should never reflect disapproval or criticism. Even if a mother tells you that sometimes she feels total rejection for her child, it is not appropriate for you to be critical of this feeling. Rather, it is necessary for you to show that you accept and are trying to understand her feelings, and that you are glad she is able to tell you about them.
- **Attentive silence.** It is important to leave enough silence for the parent to be encouraged to go on talking.
- **Giving the right encouragement.** Small acknowledgements from time to time that you have heard and understood what the parent has said, but without interrupting the flow of speech, are good encouragement. For example, you could say things like 'I see', or 'really' or even just 'mm-hm'.
- **Ask open question.** These are questions that have to be answered at length. They cannot be answered with just a 'yes' or a 'no'. For example, you could ask a parent, 'How does your child spend her day at home?' or 'How did you feel when you first learnt that your little boy had CP?'
- **Giving feedback.** Let the parent know that you have understood by summarising the answers. For example, 'I see, so your little boy spends most of his day lying on

the floor but you sometimes prop him up on a chair.' Sometimes, it may be difficult for a parent to describe a situation, and then you could ask further questions to help them give you a clearer picture. For example, 'I'm sorry I don't quite understand, do you mean...?'

It is important to be aware though, that getting a parent to talk, and listening in an open, accepting way can cause uncomfortable feelings. The parent may feel he or she is taking up too much of the therapist's time, or they may feel frustrated because the therapist is not coming up with an instant solution to their problem. The therapist, on the other hand, may be very tempted to abandon the quiet, listening approach and come in too quickly with solutions and advice. The opportunity may then be missed to hear everything the parents wanted to say, and the therapist will not have the full picture of how they manage as a family.

Coming to an agreement for action

According to the medical model, the therapist decides on a programme for the child and gives the family a list of exercises they must do with the child at home. This seldom works. A better approach is one of equal participation of the therapist and the family in the problem-solving process.

The therapist and the family each come to the situation from a very different point of view. The therapist comes with demands on the family's time and effort, besides what they have to give to their child. The therapist's concern is what might happen if the child is not given at least a minimum amount of the parent's time. It is his responsibility to achieve the best rehabilitation for the child—he will be thinking about how to prevent contractures and deformities, and how to enable the child to be as independent as possible and to achieve the best possible quality of life. The family, on the other hand, have the responsibility for the child, as well as for the family as a whole. A deal has to be struck that fits in with both these perspectives.

This process starts with open and honest sharing of information between parent and therapist. As can be seen from the diagram below, this leads to a shared definition of the problem. If the partnership is to be successful, it is important that each one understands the other's point of view.

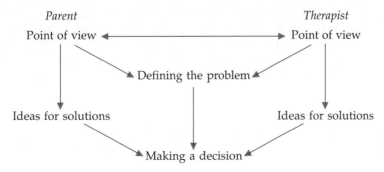

Case study

Mariam is 2 years old and has CP. She is mainly floppy, but is beginning to show some involuntary movements. She needs to be placed in good sitting and standing positions so that she can develop some postural control in an upright position. If she does not get this experience, she will start pushing herself around the floor on her back, and this will reduce her possibility of developing any hand function, and of later learning to walk.

Mariam's family are extremely poor. She lives with her 3 brothers and 2 sisters in very cramped conditions. Her father is a small-scale farmer. Her mother has been bringing Mariam to see the physiotherapist for several weeks, but it is clear that she has not been carrying out the home programme.

The physiotherapist decides to take a whole session just talking with Mariam's mother to try to negotiate a decision on how to solve the problem. At first Mariam's mother is very defensive and tries to insist that she does work hard with her daughter at home. The physiotherapist does not challenge this, but instead points out that it must be very hard for her to find time and energy to do any extra work at home. She sympathises wholeheartedly with her and shows that she understands what life must be like for her. Mariam's mother starts to cry and pours out all her concerns. Her husband gets angry because he feels she shouldn't take time to work with Mariam. He thinks Mariam will never be of any use and she should just leave her without much attention. Also, before Mariam was born, her mother used to sell some vegetables to supplement the family income. She can't do this any more because she doesn't have time. She is also too tired and depressed.

The physiotherapist realises that the mother alone cannot deal with these problems. She tells her this and then suggests that if possible, on her next visit, she should bring her husband and any other member of the family who might be willing and able to help, with her. Mariam's mother is greatly relieved to be told that the responsibility for her daughter is not hers alone.

Next week, she manages to bring her husband and his mother along. The physiotherapist finds a quiet place where they can all discuss the problem together. She then asks some open questions to the husband and mother-in-law to find out what they think about Mariam's condition, and also to learn more about the whole family's situation and ways of coping.

She discovers that Mariam's father is indeed angry about the time his wife spends with Mariam. He hints that the family income has been reduced as a result of her not being able to sell vegetables any more. The therapist also discovers that the mother-in-law has time to spend, but has the idea that Mariam's case is hopeless. (The therapist gives the family the chance to talk openly.)

Problem defined

Family's point of view: No use working on a hopeless case.
Therapist's point of view: Without work at home, the child's case will be less hopeful.

The therapist lets the family know that she understands completely what they have told her, and that she does not in any way judge or condemn their feelings and attitudes. She then tells them that she needs them to understand her point of view about Mariam. She needs them firstly to know that many children who are floppy like Mariam learn to walk in time if given some good handling early in their lives. Second, they need to understand that if Mariam is not given opportunities to be in standing and sitting, she would be much more difficult to handle and look after as she grows bigger. (The therapist expresses her opinions clearly.)

She tells them that she will help them to find ways to put Mariam in standing and sitting that will not make extra work for them. She asks them if they have any ideas on how to solve the problem of who would help Mariam's mother in carrying out Mariam's care. She explains that if Mariam is dressed in the right position, carried about in the right position, and encouraged to use her hands when playing, this would be her treatment. If everybody who handles her does these things in the right way, then in 3 months' time Mariam would, very likely, be sitting alone at least for a minute or two. (Therapist puts forward some helpful suggestions.)

The idea that there is hope for Mariam to improve and that a definite goal can be achieved, is very encouraging for the family. The grandmother immediately says she will help for an hour or two every day so that Mariam's mother could start selling vegetables again. Her father says that he would be willing to help her play whenever he is home, and would encourage the other children in the family to do the same.

Decision reached by both therapist and family

Each one is happy that what has been decided is possible and likely to be effective. Participation increases responsibility.

These suggestions were, largely, the family's own ideas. They were not imposed on them by the physiotherapist. Therefore, the family will be more likely to carry them out. Before they left, the physiotherapist showed all of them how best to lift and carry Mariam, and also some satisfying games to play with her in a good position. She told them that the next time they came, they would discuss together what kind of chair and standing frame they would find most useful so that Mariam could be placed in sitting and standing.

Being able to give information

Different people understand information they are given in different ways. Some people need to have the information written down, others understand better if the information is explained verbally and demonstrated. As therapists, we need to find out how each family member we are working with can best understand the information we are giving.

How most people learn

- If I hear it I forget it,
- If I see it I remember it,
- If I do it I know it, and
- If I discover it I own it and use it.

We have to remember that often parents feel too upset to take in any information. When a mother is in a state of shock and disbelief that her child is disabled, the only information she can take in is something that gives her hope and comfort. A way of carrying her child or positioning her that is clearly making the child less stiff or less floppy, will be the kind of information that she might be able to understand and remember. She will also be more able to accept information given to her by someone she trusts, and someone whom she knows understands her feelings and respects her as a person. In her vulnerable state, she may think that the world has a right to reject her. As therapists, we are responsible for building up her confidence in herself as a person and as a mother. We can do this by giving her only as much information as she can take in, and by helping her to act on that information.

Families are not in a state of shock all the time, however. They manage in so many ways to come to terms with their situation, and we must support them as they learn to cope. As was described in the case study, giving information to the family as a whole, rather than to just one member, is a good way of doing this. If the mother is the only person being given the information, she has the entire burden of acting on it, and of trying to convince other family members that this is the right thing to do. They may not be convinced, and then the therapist will have caused divisions in the family.

It is strange how human beings decide which information to act upon and which not! For example, we know it is bad for us to be overweight, to smoke, not to exercise or to lift things in the wrong way. But do we truthfully, always act upon this knowledge? It is interesting to reflect upon why we do not. We are more often tempted to do the things that are bad for us when we are depressed and our self-esteem is low. The same is true for families with children who have CP. They know they should do 'exercises' with their children but they are tempted to neglect this difficult duty because they don't believe they can do a good job of it. Our first duty then, is to convince them that they can, and that it will make a difference.

The information we give to the family must be just enough for them to understand exactly what we are asking them to do, and why we are asking them to do it. For example, 'If you place your child in a standing frame for 10 minutes every day, he will start to be able to balance better in sitting.' The information should also be linked to some aspect of the child's lack of ability that the family have expressed worries about. If the activity we are asking them to do is directly linked to overcoming a problem they are concerned about, they will be more likely to be motivated to carry out that activity.

Choosing short-term goals

A key to giving families hope is being able to choose short-term goals and informing the family about them. This means being able to say that some measurable improvement will happen if the programme agreed upon by the family and the therapist is carried out. An example might be of a child who pushes back into extension with any stimulation, and whose mother is having problems carrying him or leaving him in any position except supine on the floor. The programme negotiated with the family is that the child will be carried in a sitting position with no pressure against his head, and that he will be placed in a prone standing frame for 15 minutes twice a day. He will have one meal while standing in the standing frame. He will spend as much of the rest of the day as possible in a side-lying position with toys suspended so that he can touch them with his hands. The measurable improvement at the end of 6 weeks of carrying out this programme might be that the child can hold his head erect for 1 minute while he is held in a sitting position.

This small piece of improvement may not seem very impressive. However, if it has been predicted by the therapist and the programme has been faithfully carried out by the family, all concerned may be justified in feeling a sense of real achievement and be encouraged to move on to the next step.

Some families find it helpful to have a notebook in which the programme is written, and the goal they are working towards described. They might like to place a tick in a chart for every part of the programme they carry out. Over a period of a year or more, they will be pleased to look back at the number of goals they have achieved. They will also have built up a high level of confidence in their own ability to bring about improvement in the child's condition.

Example of page in home programme notebook

Date	Placed in standing	Placed in side-lying	Ate whole meal in standing
1/6	✓	✓	✗
2/6	✓	✓✓	✗
3/6	✓✓	✓✓	✗
4/6	✓	✓✓✓	✗
5/6	✓✓	✓✓	✓
6/6	✓✓	✓✓✓	✗
7/6	✓✓	✓✓	✓

The table on the opposite page could be written at the back of the same notebook so that the family can see the slow but steady progress their child is making.

Of course, it is not easy to accurately predict the child's improvement. It takes experience to know what is possible and what might be too ambitious. If you find you are being overoptimistic in your predictions, try to choose a slightly longer time or a less

Short-term goal	When set	When achieved
Sammy will be able to hold his head erect for 1 minute while he is held in sitting	3/6/99	18/7/99
Sammy will be able to lift his head and hold it up for 1 minute while lying face down over a roll	18/7/99	2/9/99
Sammy will be able to balance alone in sitting on the floor for 1 minute	2/9/99	20/10/99

difficult task. The important thing is to offer realistic hope without giving too definite promises.

Exceptionally difficult relationships

With most families, it is possible to form a working relationship that benefits the child. Sometimes, the therapist has to accept that a family cannot do as much with the child as she would like, and she has to adapt her programme to suit the family's needs and abilities. At other times, the family has to listen to the advice of the therapist so that they can make an informed choice about how to manage their child. As long as there is a close relationship between therapist and family, these issues can usually be resolved. Sometimes, however it becomes difficult to the point of being impossible to work with a family. This usually comes about because the family is under some severe strain, other than having a disabled child. The family may be living in dire poverty or one or other of the parents may be suffering from mental illness. Perhaps the family have lived through terrible experiences that have left them traumatised. On the other hand, it must be recognised that sometimes, therapists themselves become stressed and over burdened. Many hard working, conscientious therapists become burnt out because they are overwhelmed by the emotional and physical stress of the job they do. In these cases, it may help all concerned if a few weeks' break is taken from therapy. During these weeks, the therapist should have the opportunity to discuss her problems with a colleague or programme manager. Perhaps the family would do better with a new therapist for a while, or perhaps the colleague or programme manager could negotiate with the family so that a different family member works for a while with the therapist and the child.

But while everything possible must be tried for the sake of the child, sometimes it must be recognised that there is no cooperation and the relationship between the family and the therapist is one of disagreement and even hostility. Even so, it may not be necessary to give up on a family completely. Sometimes, it may be possible to get back into a relationship with them when their circumstances or access to resources change, or when they recognise their child's need for therapy. That is why it is important, even with the most unfriendly family, to try to part without harsh words so that the door is left a little open for a return to cooperation.

Table showing what family and therapist each brings to the partnership

What a family brings	*What a therapist brings*
Knowledge of the child as a person learned from the day-to-day experience of giving care.	Knowledge of how CP interferes with a child's ability to hold postures and to move normally. Ability to assess what is interfering with the child's ability to function.
Awareness of how the child is perceived in the family.	Experience of how other families have learnt to perceive children in a more positive light.
Knowledge of support available to be called upon from family members and local community.	Knowledge of what can be done to improve child's functional ability. Also, what dangers are present of contractures and deformities if the child does not receive good treatment and handling.
Lifelong commitment to the child.	Commitment to offering professional service to the child and family.
Time devoted to caring for the child—dressing, toiletting, feeding.	Ability to build the kind of relationship with the family that would enable them to work effectively with the child.
Own coping strategies for dealing with hardship and stress.	Ability to adapt the treatment programme to fit the family's circumstances.
Knowledge of local environment within which the child can find opportunities to play and interact socially with other children.	Ability to keep good records and to be able to demonstrate to the family how goals have been reached and improvement achieved.

Efforts by therapist or family each working alone will not be effective. For best results, there must be partnership.

Partnership with children

This chapter has concentrated up till now on working in partnership with the adults in a child's family. It should, however, be every therapist's ambition to draw the children themselves into the process of working in partnership. It is easy to underestimate how much even very young children understand. It can cause serious distress to a child and his family if a therapist talks about the child as if he is not there or as if he can't understand, when in fact, he understands well. This is particularly true of children who have difficulty speaking. It is a wise therapist who from the first contact with a child talks to that child in a manner that conveys a readiness to be close and to understand what the child might want to communicate. Above all, the therapist should understand every child's fundamental need to be able to play. Their CP and perhaps also their learning difficulty may be preventing them from using play in the way that normal children do to explore the world around them and to make some sense of it. The programme we decide on for each child must take this into account, and the child must be helped to play in a way that is satisfying for him.

In order to engage a child in active participation in his treatment, it is essential to choose play activities at the right level and within the intellectual capability of the child. Once the child realises that his therapist can help him to play in the way that he so longs for, he will be more ready to cooperate and work with the therapist to also achieve some of the therapist's objectives. The therapist may perhaps want the child to be placed in standing or balance in sitting, but the child may just want to play. Both can achieve their objectives if the therapist sets the scene in the right way.

Figure 6.1

The child is playing, the therapist is looking for good active extension.

Figure 6.2

The therapist has shown the child how to achieve active extension by herself.

From a very early state, a therapist can communicate to the child how it is good to be in standing: how, for example, he can see more, how tall it makes him and how strong it makes his legs. Later, when the child can understand a lot, it is very important to explain clearly why exercises are important.

Many children are, from an early age, capable of taking responsibility for some of their treatment. But this can only happen under certain conditions. The first of these conditions is that the therapist and the child's family believe the child is capable of taking responsibility, and they communicate this to him. The second is that the child feels capable and is proud of this. Choosing the right task to start the child working in this way is obviously crucial. It must be a task that the child understands to be useful. An example might be a child who spends some hours sitting at a school desk every day. To counteract this when he comes home, he does some active hip and knee extension in standing. This is a self-disciplined way of working. The child knows it helps him and he trains himself to do it. It would help if he knew of other children who work in the same way. Children who have learnt to be self-disciplined will take a great load off their parents' shoulders. They will avoid the usual ineffectual nagging that parents fall back on when things are difficult, and they will be prepared for a lifetime of understanding their condition and taking responsibility for making the best of their lives.

But all of this achievement depends on the therapist communicating in a good way with the family and the child. It depends on him choosing the right tasks for the child to take responsibility for, and finally it depends on him being able to teach the child to carry out the exercise in the right way so that the child feels good about his achievements and is motivated to continue.

Section 2

How therapy can be part of daily care

In Chapter 5, I touched on a few ways of carrying and positioning children. This chapter will cover more fully the different ways in which handling and placing children can be made easier for families. It will also show how these everyday activities can actually be treatment for the child.

Many children have to be lifted and carried around at some point in the day. Often, he or she also has to be dressed and undressed, bathed and taken to the toilet, and in between has to be left in one position or another that is safe. Some families are so stressed and busy, they may not be able to do anything more with their child than take care of these basic needs. If we can at least help them to carry out these activities in a way that is easier for them and of benefit to the child, we won't have to feel the child is getting no treatment.

The most important thing to teach the whole family is how to lift the child. Many people lift a child up from the floor as in the pictures on the opposite page.

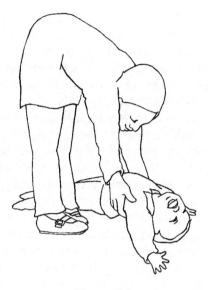

Figure 6.3

Lifting like this puts a strain on the lifter's back.

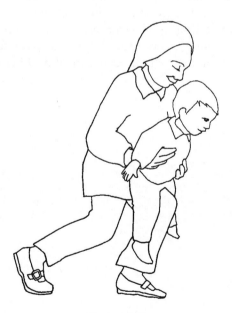

Figure 6.4

Holding the child close to the lifter's body and using her
leg muscles to lift protects her back from strain.

Lifting with straight legs and a bent back puts all the strain on the small muscles of the lifter's spine. In time, these muscles are damaged and back pain can become chronic. The secret of protecting the lifter's back is to lift in such a way that legs, rather than the back, take the strain. The child must be held close to the lifter's body, not at arms length, and the back should be kept straight while the hips and knees bend.

Most parents tend to handle children too quickly. It may be necessary to take a good deal of time to explain to them that if they handle their children more slowly and give them time to respond, they will be helping them to develop. As a child is lifted up in stages from the floor, for instance, she will try to hold her head steady in each stage. If she is just scooped up, there is no time for her to begin to take control.

Another example is when a child is dressed quickly and given no time to try to push his arm into a sleeve, or lift one foot to place in his trousers.

Teaching handling skills is an art. Often, therapists try to teach families to handle their children just by demonstrating, and parents are sometimes embarrassed to try to carry out the skill in front of the therapist. Without specific training, however, it is not possible to expect a parent to change from the way they have always handled their child to a wholly new way. Success will come only through step-by-step teaching while giving constant reassurance that they are doing a good job. But they will only be doing a good job if we have chosen the right task for them to do, and been patient and skilful in our teaching.

As you teach people these handling skills, try to remember how you felt the last time you had to learn to do something difficult. When you were a student, learning to carry out passive movements or setting up electrotherapy treatment, how easy was it to learn when your teacher was watching every move? If he was patient and encouraging, would it have been easier to learn than if he had been critical or if his body language had made him seem so?

Possible ways for carrying child

Type of CP	One way of carrying small child	Alternate way for small child	Large child
Severe Spastic Extended Child	Push back is prevented by holding hips in flexion and not supporting head	Prevents abnormal push back and facilitates postural control of head	Flexion and abduction of hips prevents abnormal push back
Severe Spastic Flexed Child	Child is held in good extension and encouraged to actively lift head	Child is held in good extension and encouraged to actively lift head	Arms are prevented from pulling down into flexion. Head and trunk encouraged to actively extend
Moderate Spastic Quadriplegia	To prevent flexor spasticity and facilitate active extension	To prevent adduction and internal rotation of hips and facilitate postural control of head and trunk	To inhibit pull down in arms
Spastic Diplegia	To prevent adduction and internal rotation of hips and facilitate postural control of head and trunk	To prevent adduction and internal rotation of hips and facilitate postural control of head and trunk	To prevent adduction and internal rotation of hips and facilitate postural control of head and trunk

(continued)

Possible ways for carrying (*continued*)*

Type of CP	One way of carrying small child	Alternate way for small child	Large child
Hemiplegia	Hemi side facing forward helps head turning to affected side	To inhibit retraction of hemi side	Child walks alone but, if insecure, hold hemi hand
Athetoid	To facilitate symmetry and postural control of head	To facilitate symmetry and postural control of head	Held in alignment for symmetry and postural control of head
Athetoid with Dystonic Spasm	To prevent extensor spasm and encourage active extension	Hips held flexed to prevent push back	To prevent extensor spasm and encourage active extension
Floppy Child	To give sensori-motor experience of upright position and facilitate postural control of head	To give sensori-motor experience of upright position	To facilitate holding head erect

*These are only suggested ways for carrying children. If they work to help the mother carry her child more easily or to help the child to have better postural control, use them. If not, try some other way.

Suggested positions in which to dress children

Type of CP	Baby	Older child	More able child
Severe Spastic Extended Child	Prevents extensor spasticity facilitates active extension	Mother's legs (one behind pelvis, one over child's legs) gives stability and leaves hands free	Child helps in dressing. Own active flexion prevents push back into extension
Severe Spastic Flexed Child	Movement of mother's legs helps prevent flexor spasticity	Encourages active extension of head and trunk from stable base	Child helps in dressing. Own active extension prevents flexor spasticity
Moderate Spastic Quadriplegia	Encourages active extension in trunk and movement of arms away from trunk	Mother's legs (one behind pelvis, other over child's legs) keeps child's hips flexed and her hands are free to help child dress	Mother's legs (one behind pelvis, other over child's legs) keeps child's hips flexed and her hands are free to help child dress
Athetoid	Flexed hips prevent push back. Neck cushion gives possibility of head in midline	Encourages active head raising and symmetry	Gives proximal fixation and possibility of dressing self

(continued)

Positions for dressing (*continued*)

Type of CP	Baby	Older child	More able child
Athetoid with Dystonic Spasm	Hip flexion prevents push back. Neck cushion gives symmetry	Prevents extensor spasms. Facilitates holding head and trunk in mid-position	Mother's legs (one behind pelvis, the other over child's legs) give proximal fixation so child can actively help
Hemiplegia	Use opportunity to get head turning to hemi side. Put hemi limbs in first	Mother sits at hemi side. Prevents neglect of hemi side and unequal weight bearing	Using hemi hand with help while holding on with unaffected hand
Floppy Child	Possibility of seeing own limbs and helping in dressing	Good position to facilitate head raising	Mother's legs (one behind pelvis, the other over child's legs) give support so child can be active in trunk and arms

It is not possible to describe the exact dressing position that is best for every kind of child. These tables are meant only to give guidelines. Try to remember that weight bearing on arms is very important and functionally useful for all children. If you can use dressing to facilitate this then try to include it in your instructions to the family. Rotation in the body axis is also very useful and helps to reduce spasticity. It is often easy to facilitate rotation while the child is prone over the mother's knees. In a more able child, shifting weight from one side to the other to lift one leg and put on a sock, for instance, is another way to facilitate rotation.

Before teaching family members about dressing the child, though, do ask them to show you how they do it themselves and ask what difficulties they have with it. If you see something going very wrong (e.g., the child becoming very asymmetric) then gently suggest, show them and let them try a different way, and explain why you think it might help the child. As a general rule choose only one thing at a time to change so that the family is not overwhelmed with the new instructions.

7

Useful equipment in a centre and at home

We use equipment for children with CP to give them opportunities to be in positions that will help them to develop better postural control, better hand function and better communication and interaction with people around them. The equipment supports the children in positions that they cannot assume and maintain themselves in, and frees the therapist's hands to work with different parts of their bodies. At home, the equipment is used for the children to gain the experience of new positions on a daily basis for half an hour or so at a time. The equipment should support the children in a way that is almost as good as we could do with our hands. The support can never be dynamic as our hand support is, but it allows the children to hold a position for longer than we or the family have time for, and allows them more freedom, independence and control.

Equipment used at therapy centre

Floor mats

Firm, padded, washable floor mats should be used for all young children. They will feel safe on these and also be free to move.

Medical plinths (padded tables)

Low plinths (not higher than 45 cm) are useful for older children and also for working with children in standing and in some sequences of movement. The medical plinths that are normally used in physiotherapy departments are too high and too narrow for young children. They serve to reinforce the perception that therapy is a medical cure: that the therapist is going to 'do something' to the child while the mother sits apart, detached from the procedure. Most children, when they are put lying on a high medical plinth, are aware of this and become fearful. These plinths should, therefore, not be used for children.

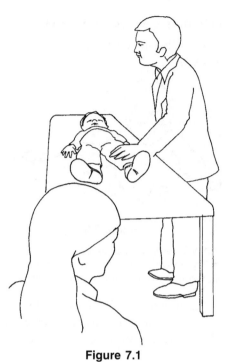

Figure 7.1

High plinth: unfriendly to mother and child.

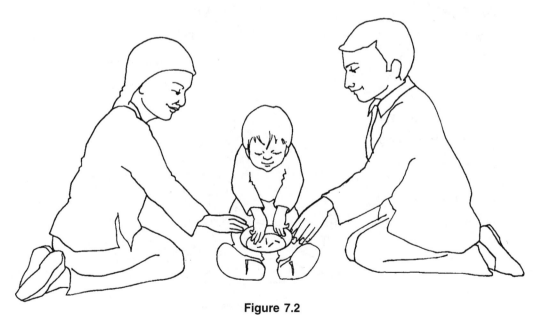

Figure 7.2

Floor mats: more natural.

Rolls (firm foam rubber cylinders covered in plastic)

Rolls are useful during treatment because they lift one part of the child's body up, and because they can be moved easily.

Figure 7.3

The lifting up of the child's body breaks up the abnormal pattern and gives her the experience of a more normal posture. The movement of the roll can further reduce spasticity, and the child can be facilitated to carry out active movements in this new position.

It is important to use the right size of roll for each child. If the roll is too small, the child may not be lifted up high enough and may not experience a useful new posture. If it is too big, the child may be lifted too high for him to be able to be active.

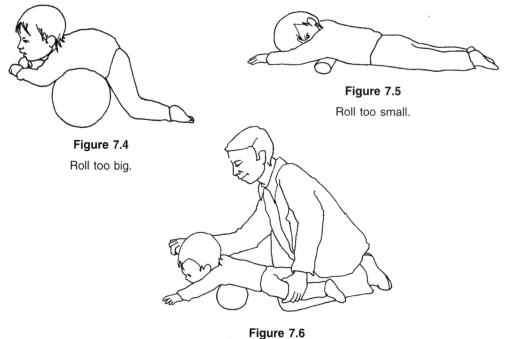

Figure 7.5

Roll too small.

Figure 7.4

Roll too big.

Figure 7.6

Roll right size.

It is always necessary to check that the roll is doing the job you want. For example, if you want to help a child to actively extend his head and trunk in prone, you might place him over a roll so that his upper trunk is supported and he can take some weight on his forearms. For some children, this will work well and your treatment will succeed in getting him to actively lift his head to look at a toy or his mother, and maybe even to reach forward with one hand as you work with his legs. For other children, however, it may have the opposite effect. The stimulation of the roll on the child's body may increase the flexor spasticity, and instead of facilitating active extension, the roll may actually reinforce the abnormal postural tone. You must constantly assess the effect on the child. If it doesn't work, don't do it.

The mobile support that rolls can provide are also useful for reducing spasticity in children with stiff pelvises.

Figure 7.7

The therapist moves the roll slightly from side to side. This reduces the spasticity in the pelvis and allows active extension and rotation in the trunk with flexion at the hips and extension in the knees.

Wedges (plastic-covered firm foam rubber)

Wedges can be used like rolls to support parts of the child's body. The difference is that a wedge is not mobile. In treatment, wedges are most useful in testing out positions in which the child may be placed at home.

For example, a child who sits on the floor with a rounded back because she cannot flex well enough at her hips, may be placed in sitting on a forward sloping wedge to see it this helps her to keep her back straighter. If it does, we can go on to experiment with different angles to see what works best. When we know the angle that works best, we can design a chair or floor cushion for the child that incorporates this angle. Other uses for wedges at home will be described later.

Figure 7.8

Using a wedge to facilitate long-sitting with a straight back.

Benches and stools

Strong, fairly heavy wooden stools and benches are essential for giving children the experience of sitting and of changing position from the floor to sitting, and from sitting to standing. Every centre should have a good selection of these so that it is possible to place children of all ages in sitting with their feet flat on the floor. Some of the bigger stools can be used as tables to find the best height for arm support for a child who is sitting, or to give the child the possibility of using his hands.

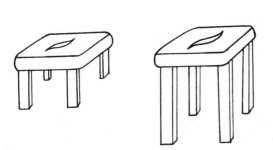

Figure 7.9

Stools varying in height from 10 cm to 60 cm—some rectangular, some square.

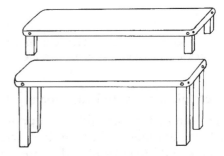

Figure 7.10

Benches varying in height from 15 cm to 30 cm, and about 1 m in length.

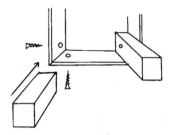

Figure 7.11

Legs should be screwed firmly to frame around seat.

The following pictures illustrate some ways in which a bench is useful.

Figure 7.12

The child sits astride on the bench so that active extension and rotation in the trunk can be facilitated, while the adduction and internal rotation of the hips are prevented.

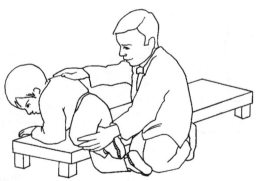

Figure 7.13

The child climbs on and off the bench while the therapist facilitates rotation of the trunk.

Figure 7.14

The child is to be supported in 'sandwich sitting': the therapist uses one leg to support the child's pelvis from the back and puts the other over the child's legs to maintain the hips in a good position while the child is active in balancing the trunk and head over this good base.

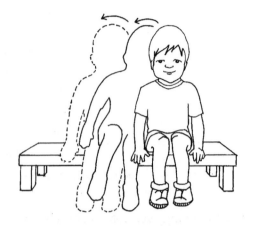

Figure 7.15

The bench is useful for a child to move sideways while sitting.

Figure 7.16

The bench is useful for a child to step on or off.

Figure 7.17

The bench is useful for a child to jump off.

Standing tables

There are electrically operated tables that can change height at the touch of a switch, but if these are not available it will be equally effective to have a carpenter make a square wooden table that has space for one or two children on each side. The table should be covered by a thin layer of sponge and then washable material. The sides of the table should be covered in the same way. Each side of the table accommodates children of different heights. On all sides there are openings for the children's feet to pass through, so that the padded side of the table can hold their knees in extension. The biggest children will have their feet flat on the floor. The smaller children will stand on stools and the openings on the sides of the table will be higher up. The aim is to place the children in a semi-supported standing position so that their feet, hips and head are in alignment. They will, most likely, need the therapist to use the pelvis as a key point of control to reduce flexion in the hips and facilitate active extension.

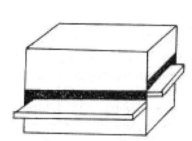

Figure 7.18

Table designed for different sized children to be supported in standing.

Figure 7.19

Children standing together at a table have the opportunity to interact and play together during therapy. It is also an opportunity for their mothers to participate in therapy and learn from the therapist and other mothers.

Walking aids

Most centres have parallel bars. But these, in the way that they encourage the children to grasp and hang on with their hands, may not facilitate active mobile weight-bearing and balance reactions in the legs and trunk. It is worth trying to replace the normal handrail with a flat plank so that, instead of grasping and pulling with his arms, the child can be facilitated to take weight on open hands and extended arms. Before he starts walking the length of the bars, it is useful to facilitate him to take steps sideways on the bars. Later, when he can balance with one foot in front of the other, he can learn to

Figure 7.20

Parallel bars with flat board instead of handrail.

shift his weight from foot to foot. In children with spasticity, this weight shift will inhibit the spasticity as long as the child is not fearful. Athetoid and ataxic children will benefit from the weight-bearing on both arms and legs, and also from experiencing the feeling of being upright and beginning to have some coordinated co-contraction in the trunk.

In addition to parallel bars, there should be walking aids to try with children who are beginning to be able to take steps. These should only be of the kind that are available for the family to take home. It is cruel to have an expensive walking aid in the centre that helps the child to walk only when she comes for exercises.

Some children, particularly athetoid and ataxic, learn to walk by pushing a fairly heavy object, e.g., a chair or a small table, in front of them. Holding on to the chair gives them symmetry and a steady point from which to move their legs. Children with spasticity need walking aids that facilitate hip extension. Walkers that the child pushes in front are more likely to facilitate hip flexion, and this will not enable him to develop balance reactions and eventually walk alone. Walkers that support the child from the back and have a ratchet on the wheels to prevent them from being a pushed backwards, *do* facilitate hip extension. Every effort should be made to develop cheap, local versions of this aid for those children who can take steps in them without their spasticity increasing.

Figure 7.21

Pushing a chair gives symmetry and fixation.

Figure 7.22

Rollator encourages child to walk with flexed hips.

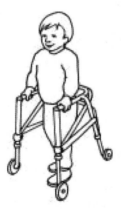

Figure 7.23

Back support walker facilitates extension of hips.

Equipment to try out

Every centre should have a selection of chairs, standing frames and walking aids available for trying out and finding the best piece of equipment for children to use at home. It takes time for a child to become used to a new position, and before sending new equipment home with a child, the therapist must be sure that the child is safe with it and also that it does the job it has been designed for. It may need several sessions to decide on the right piece of equipment and to test the child out with it.

Splints

Sometimes, it is useful to have some light splints to keep a child's limb in extension and free your hands to work on another part of his body. For example, if you are working with a child with low tone in standing, you can free your hands to help him reach by putting gaiter splints on his legs to keep his knees in extension. These can be made of fabric with lightweight metal strips incorporated to hold them straight, or, in a very young child, a few layers of newspaper fastened with sticky tape that will be just enough to stop him from collapsing.

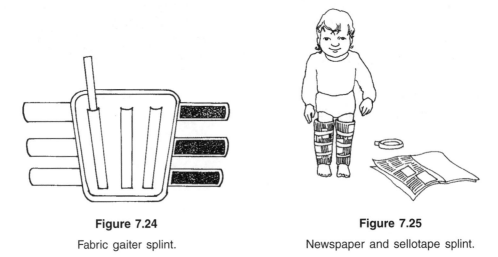

Figure 7.24

Fabric gaiter splint.

Figure 7.25

Newspaper and sellotape splint.

Toys

The right kind of toys in a therapy department has a good impact on children and their families when they first attend. Seeing other children actively playing during therapy motivates both the child and his family to be actively involved themselves. A broken doll and a therapist desperately snapping his fingers to attract a child's attention are very poor substitutes.

It is very important to keep the toys in a cupboard and to only take out what is needed for any child at any one time. Too many toys at once can be distracting and counter-productive. The right containers for toys are also important so that all the toys do not end up in a jumble of mixed-up pieces. Jigsaw puzzles need to be kept separate with all their pieces intact. A set of blocks should be kept in one container, a set of objects especially collected for texture in another. Toys that are broken or incomplete should be repaired or thrown away.

In Appendix B there is a table of play activities during therapy for children at different stages of development.

Figure 7.26

A tidy, well-arranged toy cupboard shows that therapists understand the
need for children to play and the value of using play in therapy.

Equipment used at home

In parts of the world where there are few therapists, children may have little chance of a
full rehabilitation programme. They may, however, have the possibility of receiving a
piece of equipment to use at home. It is, therefore, of crucial importance that therapists
and community workers know how to,

- choose the right kind of equipment in partnership with the family,
- make sure the equipment fits the child well,
- explain to the family the way in which the equipment will help the child, and to
- make sure the family know how to prepare the child before placing her in the equipment, and also how long she should spend in it and how active she should be.

Equipment that will be used by a child at home must be very carefully chosen. It is not
just the very important issue of how it may or may not help the child that needs to be
considered. It is also the question of how it may be received by the family. Will they see
it as something that is helpful to them in the way they care for the child? Is there room
enough for it in the house? Will it be very difficult for them to position the child in it?
Time needs to be taken to discuss these issues with the family. If a mother has asked for
a chair so that she doesn't always have to feed her child sitting on her lap, then she will
be more likely to use the chair when she gets it. If a therapist decides (for the best possible

reasons) that a child needs a standing frame, but he hasn't taken time to discuss the situation with the family and explain why it may help their child, then he must not blame the family if they decide not to use it.

It has been observed that families who have opportunities to learn how to make their own equipment, use that equipment with pride and confidence. Of course, not everyone can have this opportunity, but if the family are given the chance to share in the decision about what kind of equipment is best and how it should look, they will have a sense of ownership of it. They will value it more than if it is just handed over to them because the therapist thinks it is a good idea.

One of the most difficult issues is deciding which piece of equipment will be the most useful. Most families will ask for a chair because it is easy to imagine how they and the child will benefit from the child being in a safe, comfortable sitting position. The trouble with sitting, however, is that it can fix the child in quite a lot of flexion, and it gives no opportunity for weight-bearing on the legs. In addition, it can be difficult, without complicated adaptations to the chair, to use the sitting position to give the child all he needs. On the one hand, he needs to learn to balance his trunk on his pelvis, to be symmetrical, and to have a good base from which to use his hands. On the other, his mother needs him to be in a position in which she can easily feed him, and where she can leave him for a while knowing he is safe and comfortable while she gets on with other work.

A standing frame may be able to give the child all of these things more easily than a chair. It is more likely that he will be symmetrical in it, he can bear weight on his legs, he has good opportunities to balance his trunk on his pelvis and, if he has a table in front, he can use his hands. For many children, even eating and drinking can be easier in a standing frame than in a chair. Most importantly, the majority of children are happier to be in standing at least for short periods.

But this is a strange idea for many families and it may take time and sensitive persuasion before they can accept it. It may be necessary to give them a chair at home at first and to demonstrate in the centre over a number of weeks how the standing frame may be better. If they live in a very small house and have only room for one piece of equipment, they will need to be totally convinced of the benefit of the standing frame before they will be ready to give up the chair. Of course, most children will benefit from having both a chair and a standing frame.

Every piece of equipment must be safe for the child to use. It must be carefully explained to the family that a child must not be left for too long (usually not more than half an hour) in any position, and that he should not be left alone, particularly in standing frames.

The following are some pieces of equipment that might be useful for families to have at home:

Wedges

These are useful for positioning a child for short periods. Those children who are able to lift their heads a little when placed in prone over a wedge may benefit from this as long as they are left with toys within reach. The family must be sure, however, that the child will not roll over and fall off. If there is any danger of this, sandbags can be placed on either side of the child.

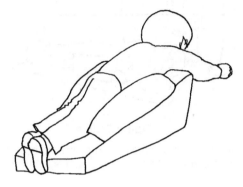

Figure 7.27

Prone over wedge supported with sandbags.

Children in danger of hip dislocation because of the adduction and internal rotation of their hips when they are left lying supine, may benefit from having their legs flexed over a wedge. This breaks up the pattern of spasticity and also gives them symmetry.

Children who push back into extension when they lie on their backs may benefit from having their nappies changed lying on a low wedge. The wedge should flex their hips just enough to inhibit the spasticity.

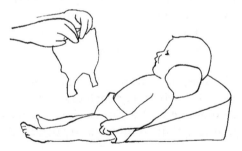

Figure 7.28

Wedge giving hip flexion to reduce push-back into extension.

Side-lying board

This is useful for children who are very floppy. It is also useful for those children who push back into extension when they are left supine, but who cannot tolerate being left in prone.

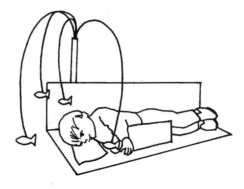

Figure 7.29

The side-lying position gives children symmetry and allows them to bring their hands together in front of their eyes. It is helpful to have some toys suspended near their hands.

The board can be made of cardboard or wood. If it is made of wood, it should be covered with a thin layer of sponge and washable fabric. The front support should be high enough to prevent the child from rolling into supine, but small enough to allow free movement of her arms. It should be in the middle of the board so that sometimes the child can be placed on her right side and sometimes on her left. She should always have a small firm pillow under her head.

Chairs (special seating)

In countries with adequate resources, chairs which can be adapted to all kinds of children are often available. They can be changed to allow the child to relax in them or to be active in them. They 'grow' with the child, and can be easily moved around. Even so, because they are so expensive, it is not easy for every child to have the right chair exactly when it is needed. In this book, we only have space to describe chairs that are simple in design and easily reproduced.

The following are descriptions of a selection of chairs that can be made of appropriate paper-based technology (APT) or wood. For each one, there are suggestions as to which children may benefit from them and why. The designs for making them from APT and the way of taking measurements will be found in Appendix A.

Reclining chair

This is modelled on the small chair used for normal babies. It supports the child in a reclining position, upright enough so that she can see what is going on around her, but not so upright that she is in any danger of flexing forwards.

These chairs are useful for children with very low tone. They give them the possibility of being a little upright and, if they have a table in front at chest height, of perhaps being able to use their hands. A neck pillow may be needed to help keep the child's head in midline, and a foot-board will help to give support to this feet.

Figure 7.30

Neck cushion elongates neck
and prevents extension.

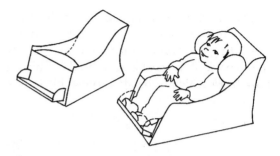

Figure 7.31

Reclining chair showing neck cushion
and foot-board.

For older children with severe spasticity too, this chair is useful, especially for feeding. If the chair back is slightly curved from side to side, the child will be more comfortable and may be able to tolerate a more upright position than if the back is flat. It is important to make sure that the child's pelvis is right back in the seat. Groin straps may be needed to keep the pelvis back, and also to keep the hips outwardly rotated. A padded post between his legs would not be so good because the child is likely to push against it using abnormal extension, and this will increase his adductor spasticity.

Figure 7.32

Groin straps must be fastened at the right angle to outwardly rotate the hips.

Upright chair and table

Children who have some head and trunk control should be in upright chairs rather than reclining chairs. This is because they need the experience of being upright so that they can begin to hold the position for themselves. If a child has quite low tone and falls forward, or if there is some pulling down into the flexion pattern in his arms, the table should be at chest height.

This kind of chair is useful for children with moderate spastic quadriplegia. Make sure that his pelvis is not pulled back more on one side than on the other, and that he is not sitting back on his sacrum. It may be necessary to use knee blocks to push his pelvis to the back of the seat and to hold his hips in some abduction. This will give him a good base from which to be able to use his hands.

Figure 7.33

Upright chair showing table at chest height and knee blocks.

Prone angle (forward tilting) chair

Children with poor trunk control who go into total extension pattern when they lift their heads, have great difficulty sitting in an upright chair. As soon as they lift their heads, their arms lift up into abduction and outward rotation, and they cannot bring them forward on to the table. These children need to be in a forward-tipped sitting position supported at chest height from the front.

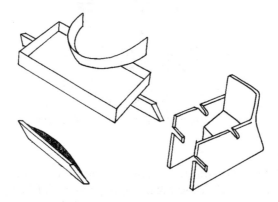

Figure 7.34

The forward-tipped position reduces extensor spasticity.

In this position, when they lift their heads, there is nothing to push against and they are not likely to go into total extension. Their weight is tipped forward by the sloping seat so that they take weight on their knees against the knee blocks and on the chest support. Their hands can then come forward on to the table.

The benefit of this position is that the child is not strapped tightly in the chair. The curved chest support allows just enough movement for the child to learn some postural control, but not enough to allow him to slump in any direction. The angle of the seat of the chair is critical. Too far forward and it may be difficult for him to lift his head at all, too far back and he is in danger of pushing backwards again. Getting it right needs a lot of experimenting, but having a chair like this may save many athetoid children from trying to fix themselves using their arms or legs because of the poor co-contraction in their trunk. Without such a chair, an athetoid child can develop strong flexor spasticity in arms and legs, and these can lead to painful contractures and deformities in later life.

Standing frames

All through this book there has been a strong emphasis on the need to give children with CP opportunities to take weight on their legs. Being in a standing position can give a child more possibility of symmetry and alignment, of learning postural control, of avoiding contractures and deformities and of being in a position that is enjoyable and satisfying. It is not possible for family members to hold a child in a good standing position for more than 5 or 10 minutes at a time. This is not long enough for the child to benefit much. He may need half an hour two or three times a day depending on how much he enjoys it, and on how necessary it may be to prevent him from being in more harmful positions such as W-sitting or crawling.

There are two main kinds of standing frame that are useful for children with CP:

- a prone angle (forward tilting) standing frame, and
- an upright standing frame.

In some centres, standing frames which support the child from behind (supine standers) are used. In these, the child leans backwards in the standing position. *These are not recommended.* The reason is, first of all, that it does not feel at all normal for the child but, second and more important, in order to reach forward with her hands and to look at what she is doing, she must actively *flex* in her hips and trunk. Children with CP who are trying to learn to stand, need to develop active hip *extension* against gravity. So, supine standing frames actually encourage the *wrong* action.

Prone angle standing frames, on the other hand, tip the child forward slightly so that every time he lifts his head and trunk and uses his hands, he may be facilitated to actively extend his hips. This does though, depend very much on the standing frame supporting him in just the right way. The points to check carefully are:

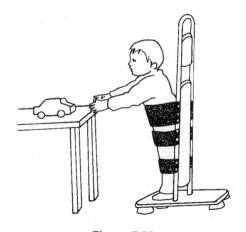

Figure 7.35

Supine standing frame.

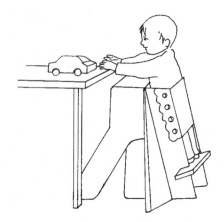

Figure 7.36

Prone angle standing frame.

- Does the pelvic belt hold the hips in extension so that the child's head, hips and heels are in alignment? This will depend on the side supports being just the right width. If they are too wide, the child's hips will flex inside the belt and there will be no possibility of active hip extension. If they are too narrow, the belt will hold the child too tightly and he will just hang on the belt, and again there will be no active hip extension.

Figure 7.37

Side supports too wide.

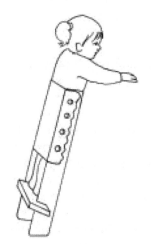

Figure 7.38

Too narrow.

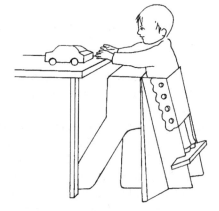

Figure 7.39

Just right.

- The angle of the frame should be upright enough so that the child can actively extend his head and trunk, but not so upright that he has no need to actively extend.

There are many adaptations that can be made to a standing frame that will help to achieve the best position and active movement in the child.

(a) If the child stands in the frame with his legs in adduction and internal rotation, a small block can be built into the frame at the level of his knees. This should be just enough to prevent adduction but not to place his legs in too much abduction. This is because abduction, being part of the flexion pattern, will make flexion in his hips and knees more likely.
(b) Athetoid children very often only take weight on one leg in standing. They may flex the other leg and then be in danger of slipping down through the belt if the weight-bearing leg collapses. They need heel cups to prevent them flexing, and maybe also foot-straps to keep both feet flat.

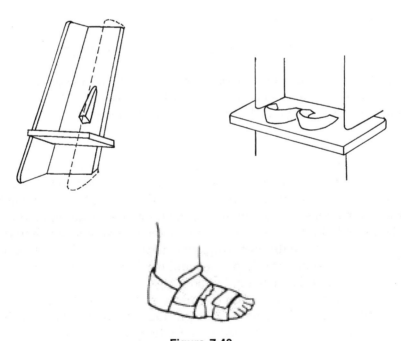

Figure 7.40

Abduction block and heel cups (foot-straps can be added).

(c) Dystonic children may suddenly push back into extension when standing in the frame. They may even push the whole frame over backwards. To prevent this, an extension can be made to the pelvic belt with long straps around the shoulders that fasten to the table in front. This will keep the shoulder girdle protracted (pulled forwards) and prevent a full extensor thrust.

Figure 7.41

Straps to keep shoulder girdle from pushing backwards.

Standing frames can be made of APT or of wood. If they are made of wood, they will need the front panel covered in sponge and washable material. This should not be too thick or soft; otherwise the child's knees will be able to flex into it.

Preparing the child

A great deal of care needs to be taken in putting a child into a standing frame. If she has spasticity, this should first be reduced, and then the child should be lifted into the frame without losing the good position. Some toys should be placed on the table beforehand so that, if she is apprehensive, she will have something to take her mind off her worries. The pelvic belt should be fastened first, and *later* the foot-straps and shoulder straps, if they are needed. *Never* fasten the foot-straps first, in case the child should have a sudden extensor thrust and fall out. If this happened and her feet were fixed, she would be very likely to have a fractured tibia or fibula in both legs.

Upright standing frames are useful for children who have good head and trunk control, but cannot stand alone for long without using their hands for support. Being in the standing frame makes them accustomed to not relying on their hands (see Figures 7.42 and 7.43).

Care should be taken, however, in deciding on an upright standing frame. Remember that in order for a child to be able to stand alone, he needs good active extension in his hips and knees. If he is not getting opportunities to actively extend his hips and knees in

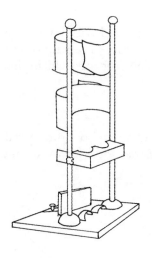

Figure 7.42

Upright stander.

Figure 7.43

Active extension of hips.

the upright stander, then he is not getting good preparation for standing alone. Some children may hang on to the belts of the stander and actively extend only in the lumbar spine. Check this is not the case before you decide.

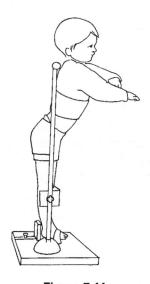

Figure 7.44

Extension of lumbar spine—no active extension in hips.

An upright standing frame can be made of wood or metal with wide vinyl straps and velcro fastening to support the pelvis and chest. The knees are supported by padded, curved wooden blocks just below the knee joint. The feet are held by heel cups and straps.

Inserts

In wheelchairs and pushchairs, children need to be given good sitting positions so that they will be comfortable and so that they can use the opportunity to develop better postural control.

Figure 7.45

Poor sitting position in pushchair.

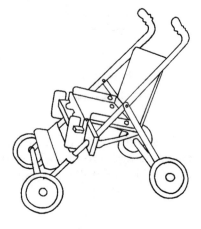

Figure 7.46

Insert attached to pushchair.

Rather than making complicated systems of straps that family members may find tiresome to fasten, APT inserts may hold the child in a good position. For example, a child who sits back on his sacrum and has windswept hips in sitting, could have an insert with knee blocks in his wheelchair.

A child who pushes back into extension could have a prone angle insert with chest support in her pushchair.

Figure 7.47

Improved sitting position of child.

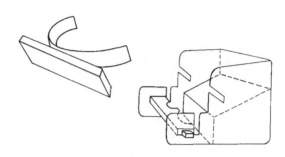

Figure 7.48

Prone angle insert for pushchair.

Ride-on walkers

Children who move around on the floor either in crawling with too much flexion, or pushing themselves along on their backs, are in danger of contractures and deformities, and also of not developing good function either in their arms and hands or in their legs. Alternative means of moving around are necessary. Let me first of all say that baby walkers are *not* acceptable. This is because they support the child in such a way that he can use his spasticity to push himself about, or, if he is athetoid or ataxic, he is given no opportunity to develop postural control and uses asymmetrical movements to get about. Also, most children with CP learning to walk are taller than the one-year-old babies that walkers are designed for. This means that they will, therefore, walk with very flexed legs if they use such walkers. The following are more appropriate suggestions:

(a) *Tricycle with the pedals cut off.* This is a useful aid for a child who has good enough balance to sit alone on. It should be high enough to allow him to push himself along using his feet on the ground without his legs being too bent. At first, he will push himself backwards using both feet, but later, with some help, he will learn to go forwards and maybe use his feet reciprocally. Take care not to choose a tricycle with a very wide seat because then his legs will be in too much abduction and it will be hard for him to extend them. For older children, it may be possible to use a bicycle with trainer wheels.

For children whose sitting balance is not reliable, it may be possible to attach a trunk support ring to the tricycle.

Figure 7.49

Using legs on the floor to propel tricycle.

Figure 7.50

Trunk support ring attached to tricycle.

(b) *Munster horse.* This is a wooden horse on 4 castor wheels that can move freely in any direction and is easy to make. The seat is narrow and can be covered with a firm cushion shaped to keep the child's legs in some abduction and outward rotation. The seat and handles can be moved up as the child grows. It would be useful for a child who has good sitting balance.

Figure 7.51

Munster horse.

(c) *APT wheeled walkers*. It is difficult to find suitable walkers for athetoid children, particularly those with dystonic spasms. Since the main problem with many athetoid children is that they do not have adequate co-contraction and stability in the trunk, they tend to compensate for this by fixing the upper parts of their body in extreme positions in order to move their legs. I have seen children in home-made large baby walker-type equipment careering around a room having such good fun. The problem is that they either flex their trunk forward or push back into extension, and then use head movement (ATNR) to take steps. Since it is so important for a child to be able to move, it is worthwhile making equipment that will help him to do this in a good way. The APT walker supports his trunk in just the right way, so that he can learn to move his legs and take steps at the same time as developing some coordinated co-contraction in his trunk.

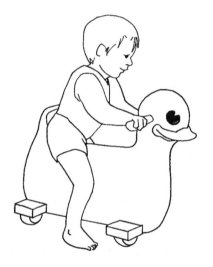

Figure 7.52

Walker with no trunk support.

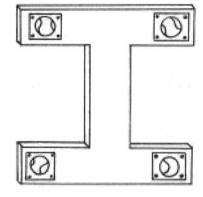

Figure 7.53

The base of this walker is wood. It is fitted with 4 castors so that it can move in any direction.

The walker has a rather narrow, slightly rounded sitting base so that the child's legs are slightly abducted and outwardly rotated. She can sit either on the base itself, or a more supportive saddle can be made. She leans forward on to a curved chest support with a fairly broad strap fastened with velcro across her back. She can hold on with her hands if this is possible, but with many athetoid children this may be difficult. If her arms have strong dystonic spasms, a wide, shawl-type band can be placed around her shoulders and arms and fastened to the front of the walker. This may seem rather restrictive, but at least it will give a child with these difficult spasms the possibility of using her fairly good legs for weight-bearing, moving around and having fun.

Figure 7.54

Shoulder straps to inhibit dystonic spasms and give child fixed base from which to move.

Toilet chairs

Having a child learn to be clean and dry is one of the most important things for any family. Children with CP may have extra difficulties with learning this because of the problems they have with maintaining positions. They may be fearful when placed on a toilet or pot because their balance is unreliable or because they cannot sit comfortably.

Normally, a child will squat to pass urine or faeces. This position is the most effective one for using the abdominal muscles to empty the bowel. But for children with CP, squatting is very difficult because it is such a flexed position. In order to balance, they need to be lifted up off the ground a little. This can be done on a child's pot which has a wide base; or the child can have a special chair, made from wood or APT, with a plastic covering on the seat (see Figures 7.55 and 7.56).

When the child is first learning to use the toilet or a pot, he will need to be held securely by his mother so that he can feel safe. Once he has learnt how to pass urine or faeces in the pot and he is confident about it, he can start learning to balance more on his own. If he has some sitting balance but needs to hold on with his hands, the pot can be placed inside a cardboard box which has a bar across it that he can hold. The sides of the box and the bar to hold will give him security (see Figure 7.57).

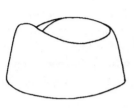

Figure 7.55

Steady, wide-based pot.

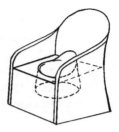

Figure 7.56

Toilet chair.

Figure 7.57

Pot inside cardboard box.

If, however, he is the kind of child who pushes back all the time, he may need to be supported from the front. If he already has a forward-tilting chair, perhaps this could be adapted to also be a toilet chair. A hole could be cut in the seat and the remaining surface could be covered in strong washable plastic. A flat board could be placed over the hold when he uses the chair other than in the toilet.

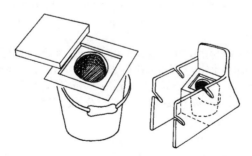

Figure 7.58

Adapted forward-tilting chair.

Bathing aids

Most children enjoy the experience of being bathed. This is true, however, only if they feel safe. When the child is fairly small and if he has some sitting balance, he will feel safe in a bath-tub as long as someone is close by. If he is the kind of child who sits back on his sacrum and whose upper back is rounded, he will be helped by sitting up on a semi-inflated swimming ring. It one does not help him enough, try two tied together.

Figure 7.59

Sitting on a semi-inflated ring may give a child just enough support to help him learn to balance.

Until a child has good sitting balance, it is helpful for him to have a towel to sit on. This gives him a less slippery surface to balance on.

The child whose sitting balance is not so good will need some support while being bathed. If the mother is doing this alone, she must either hold on to the child with one hand and wash him with the other, or use a special support in which she can place him and know he will be safe.

It is important to help the family member who bathes the child to find a good position to be in, so that they can hold the child safely but not damage their own backs. Kneeling on a soft cushion is usually better than stooping over. If kneeling is difficult, sitting on a low stool may be an alternativev (see Figures 7.60 and 7.61).

Shower aids

For bigger children, showering is easier than bathing. If the child has no sitting balance but does not push back too much into extension, then a reclining chair made of plastic pipes may be the answer (see Figure 7.62).

Figure 7.60

Stooping over child is damaging
for mother's back.

Figure 7.61

Sitting on a low stool is better.

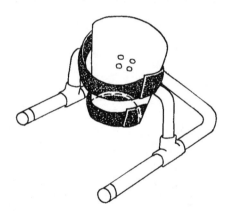

Figure 7.62

Supporting chair made of plastic pipes.

If the child does push back into extension and cannot be made comfortable in such a chair, a side-lying support may be the answer (see Figure 7.63).

Children who can balance alone while sitting on a chair will benefit from having a plastic chair with wide openings that is just the right size for them in the shower. They can use the opportunity to practise standing up and sitting down, especially if there is a firm handrail for them to hold on to. They can also start to learn to wash themselves (see Figures 7.64 and 7.65).

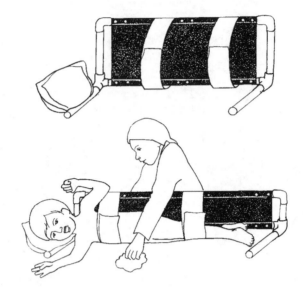

Figure 7.63

Side-lying support made of PVC pipes.

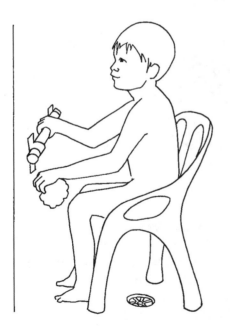

Figure 7.64

A light plastic chair that is the right height is good for a child to use in the shower.

Figure 7.65

Hand over hand learning to wash herself.

8

Assessment and management of eating and drinking difficulties

Marian Browne

Many children with CP have eating and drinking difficulties. These range from relatively minor difficulties in coordination of oral movements causing eating to be slow and with excessive spillage, to severe incoordination of the swallowing mechanism, causing ill health and even life threatening conditions. Mealtimes may stretch up to 15 times longer than for other children (Gisel and Patrick, 1988) and even despite this lengthy eating time, the children often do not receive adequate nourishment. Bax (1989) found that 20 per cent of the children with CP in his study were severely underweight or badly nourished due to eating and drinking problems. This represented half the children who had eating and drinking problems.

For most of us, eating and drinking is a pleasure, and an important opportunity to meet socially with friends and family. Feeding times form a vital part of the bonding process which occurs between mother and the young infant. As the child grows, mealtimes provide opportunities to learn communication and social skills. The child with CP who has difficulty eating may have very negative experiences of mealtimes. Carers are often anxious about ensuring adequate food intake for their child, and this anxiety frequently interferes with healthy communication and feeding practices. Experiences of coughing and choking may be frequent and very frightening for many children with eating difficulties and their carers. It is common for children to show a strong aversion to mealtimes. In addition, as many as 75 per cent of all children with CP may experience some degree of gastro-oesophageal reflux* which itself may cause chronic and severe pain (Rempel et al., 1988).

Eating and drinking problems are often found to be the major cause of concern for parents of children with CP. If managed poorly, they may worsen over time and cause ill health. However, appropriate handling of children at mealtimes and careful management of food and feeding techniques can minimise these harmful symptoms and sometimes prevent them from occurring (Larnert and Ekberg, 1995; Gisel et al., 1996).

The development of eating and drinking

In order to recognise and understand difficulties in eating and drinking, it is important to have a sound understanding of the normal processes involved, and the way in which eating and drinking skills develop in the young infant and child. Mothers will recognise that the well-being of young babies is dependant on the quality of their feeding: how readily they take milk, how much they take at a time, whether they have indigestion, 'colic' or reflux, and whether they can establish a regular pattern of feeding and sleeping. Difficulties at this stage may be the first indication of an abnormality in the developmental process.

The normal eating and drinking process is made possible by the presence of a number of protective and adaptive reflexes which include the cough, gag, suck, swallow and chewing reflexes.

Adaptive reflexes

Babies are known to swallow from the twelfth week of gestation or earlier (Humphrey, 1970). The healthy baby is usually able to locate a nipple or teat by his **rooting reflex**. This enables the baby to turn his mouth to the source of touch on his face, and to latch on to it to begin sucking. Although there is great variation in the way in which babies suck and swallow, healthy babies are able to suck in a rhythmical pattern, and to coordinate this with regular breathing. Although some coughing may occur, it is very occasional. The coordination of sucking, breathing and swallowing is smooth, and the baby automatically stops breathing momentarily during a swallow. The speed and strength of sucking will be determined by the baby's degree of hunger, level of arousal, milk supply and so on.

The **suck-swallow reflex** is usually elicited by rooting The infant moves his tongue vigorously in a forward and backward pattern and swallows regularly after each suck. From about 3 months, this pattern is gradually modified to a more mature suck which involves elevation of the tongue tip. The baby begins to be able to swallow without a prior suck.

Protective reflexes

There are two protective reflexes, the cough and the gag, which are present at birth. The **gag reflex** prevents the baby from taking anything too large or otherwise dangerous into the digestive system, and causes the tongue and pharyngeal muscles to eject the food forwards into the mouth (a kind of 'reverse peristalsis'). The **cough reflex** is triggered by something actually entering the airway or entrance to it. It causes a sharp breath outwards to expel the foreign material or build-up of secretions. The cough reflex is the body's most important protection for the airway during eating and drinking.

Weaning

In Britain, from 3–4 months, babies are introduced to semi-solid or puréed food on a spoon. The baby is supported in a sitting position and is usually able to keep her head stable. Initially food is sucked from the spoon, with a forward and backward tongue movement, with quite a lot of food being pushed out of the mouth during this process. The feeder helps the baby remove the food from the spoon by tipping the spoon up. Gradually, the baby's tongue starts to move in a more upwards and downwards direction in the mouth, and the lips become more effective in removing food from the spoon.

From 3 months, the baby begins to enjoy putting her own hands in her mouth. Soon she is able to hold toys and clothes to her mouth too, and by 5 months, she also enjoys sucking her own toes. For the majority of waking hours, the infant explores the environment through this 'mouthing' process, which plays an important part in the development of self-awareness and body-image. It is recognised to be an important part of the development of oral skills, and through this process children develop control of their tongue, lips and jaw, and learn to recognise a variety of different sensations.

By 6 months old, the infant is beginning to sit quite well, and has good head control. This provides the essential background of **stability** that makes possible the development of chewing and babbling. When the head is stable, the infant's tongue can begin to move separately from the jaw, and more complex patterns of mouth movements are possible.

The beginnings of **chewing** can be seen at about 5 months. To begin with, pressure on the infant's gums elicits a regular up-and-down biting or 'munching' pattern on a hard toy or fingers. If something is placed to the sides of the mouth, the tongue will move to touch it by a kind of 'rooting'. Once a piece of food is softened by munching, it moves on to the centre of the tongue and can be sucked. At this stage, it is not safe to give a baby, hard foods to chew, since small pieces of solid food in the mouth may cause choking.

The baby's ability to move the tongue sideways increases, and from 7 to 9 months, a rotatory movement of the jaw can be seen when food is held in the mouth. At first, the food is 'held' between the teeth, and hands are used to break the food into manageable pieces. By 12 months, the baby can use the tongue to move food from the centre to the sides of the mouth for chewing. By 2-years-old, a hard bite can be sustained with the jaw. The head may still be tilted, and hands used to break off something very hard, such as a piece of carrot.

As the young baby develops, the use of lips to actively remove food from the spoon becomes more apparent. By 18 months, chewing whilst keeping lips closed (to keep all the food in the mouth) is possible, although some spillage and dribbling is common up to about 2 years. The occurrence of mouth closure during chewing tends to be determined by the cultural environment. During swallowing, the lips are closed from early infancy.

The introduction of babies to **drinking** from a cup varies enormously, although for many in Western Europe, it begins at the same time as the introduction of semi-solid food. Cups with a spout are usually used at first, so that the baby can use the forward-backward sucking pattern effectively to take fluid from the cup. The tongue may protrude beneath the cup to provide some stability, and then the child may learn to bite on the edge of the cup to keep it stable. As the child's control of lip and jaw movements develops, the flow of fluid from an open cup is controlled by lips. By 2 years, a more mature drinking pattern is apparent, and the jaw is held still without biting the cup.

Normal eating and drinking patterns

In order to recognise and effectively treat eating and drinking problems, we need to understand the way in which we normally take food into our mouths, chew and swallow it. It is helpful to consider this process in three stages: the pre-oral stage, the oral stage and the swallow.

The pre-oral stage

Before we take food into our mouths we would normally have our mouths lightly closed, with jaw and lips together, but with no contact between the teeth. The tongue rests in the lower jaw, possibly lightly touching the teeth. Saliva production is minimal and we swallow the saliva we produce regularly, but without thinking about it.

As the food approaches the mouth, there would usually be a slight increase in the amount of saliva produced. The lips 'purse' or move forward slightly, and the lower jaw opens just enough to allow the food to be placed in the mouth. This graded movement of the lips and jaw is regulated finely and timed perfectly to 'greet' the approaching food, as we monitor visually the food intake. The lips seal around the food to control intake, and hold it in as the utensil is removed, or as we bite food off.

The oral stage

Once the food is in our mouths, we keep our heads in a stable position. The chin is tucked in and the back of the neck is always elongated to give the airway the maximum protection against food going down the wrong way. Whatever position the body assumes, whether standing, sitting, or reclining, elongation of the back of the neck is maintained because it is essential for safety in swallowing.

Food in the mouth is controlled by the tongue, cheeks and lips working together. The inside of the mouth has fine sensory awareness which enables the tongue to locate food, move it to the sides and to keep it between the biting surfaces of the teeth for chewing. Chewing usually comprises a mixture of up-and-down, side-to-side and rotatory jaw movements. If the texture of food is mixed, we swallow the runny components, and then chew the remaining more solid texture. These selective movements of the tongue, lips and jaw all depend on the jaw being stable, and able to act as a support for the finely graded movements that are needed for chewing.

If the texture and quantity of food in the mouth requires it, we may close our lips during chewing to prevent food or fluid from falling out. This use of our lips depends on sensory feedback from within and around the mouth. Breathing patterns are carefully regulated during eating so that we will usually exhale after taking food into the mouth as safety measure against any particles being inhaled into the airway.

The swallow

When food is ready to be swallowed, we close our lips, and suck the food on to the centre of the tongue. Once food is held on the tongue, with lips still closed, we push it to the back of the mouth by lifting up the tongue tip, and then, gradually, the body of the tongue. When food reaches the back of the tongue, the pressure of the food on the sides of the pharynx triggers off the swallow reflex which ensures that the airway is protected as food passes over the entrance to the larynx, and that breathing momentarily stops.

Assessment of eating and drinking patterns in the child with CP

The presence of abnormal tone and altered oral sensory awareness in the child with CP gives rise to typical abnormal eating and drinking patterns. These patterns can be understood by analysing the nature and distribution of postural tone. Appropriate management through handling, variation of the nature of food and fluid given, and therapeutic feeding techniques can then be implemented in accordance with this analysis.

It is helpful to look at typical problems which can be recognised in the three stages described below.

Pre-oral stage

Children who have eating and drinking difficulties often feel very anxious about mealtimes. Eating may be associated with excessive bouts of coughing or choking which are frightening. In many cases where children suffer from gastro-oesophageal reflux (food coming up from the stomach), eating may be painful. Many children with severe eating difficulties may never be able to eat enough to satisfy their hunger.

The approach of food to the mouth, or the mere presentation of it before the child, may cause a significant increase in the occurrence of abnormal patterns of movement. The presentation of food arouses all the senses: vision, hearing, smell and touch, in addition to the emotions. This high level of stimulation causes an increase in postural tone, involuntary movements, or the occurrence of spasms, and this in turn will impede the functional process of eating or drinking. The following should be assessed:

Position

Evaluation of the child's position is perhaps the most important part of the clinician's assessment of the eating and drinking process. The position of the child is the central factor which influences all other aspects of eating and drinking.

Is the child supported in a stable sitting or standing position? Is the trunk sufficiently stable to support the head? Is the spine extended and well aligned? Can the child maintain an elongated back of neck during the eating and drinking process, or can this position be facilitated by handling and/or provision of supportive equipment?

It is important that the child is comfortable at mealtimes, and that the position assumed should not require constant effort to sustain. It is also important for the child to be able to monitor the approach of food visually, and to be able to make eye contact with the person assisting during mealtime. Vision plays an important role in the accurate control of the timing and grading of jaw, lip and tongue movements in taking food or fluid into the mouth.

Jaw

Does the jaw provide a stable basis for movements of the tongue, cheeks and lips? How does it move, and why does it move in this way?

Where increased tone is apparent, the jaw may be retracted (pulled back), associated with extension of the neck. If there is severe spasticity, the jaw may hardly open or move at all. It may open too far (compare to the opening of our mouths which is exactly graded to the size of food that is to be eaten). Where tone is low or fluctuating, the jaw may open and close excessively. In some cases, it may be pulled to one side or the other in association with increases in tone, or in cases of excessive involuntary movements.

Lips

Is the child able to use lips to remove food from a spoon, control fluid pouring from a cup, or to keep food in the mouth? If the lips are passive (not moving enough), then it is important to know the reason for this. Is the tone in the lips high or low? It may be necessary to feel the lips to find this out. Can the child actually feel the food with his lips? In many cases, the mouth opens too widely for the lips to respond to the presence of food; that is to say, the lips are unable to function adequately due to a lack of jaw stability which would normally give them a stable basis from which to work.

Tongue

Where does the tongue lie in the mouth when at rest? Can the tongue be still? Is it pulled back or to one side in association with increased tone? Often, the tongue moves forward and backward in conjunction with opening and closing of the jaw. This may sometimes be described as a 'tongue thrust' when the tongue protrudes beyond the lips. It may occur when there is no food in the mouth, and will be more marked when the child uses effort. This pattern of tongue movement stems from a lack of stability of the jaw.

Can the tongue move food to the sides of the mouth in order for it to be chewed? In many cases, the tongue moves only from front to back, and lacks lateral movements.

As a child prepares to eat or drink, there is normally an increase in saliva production. The child who has oral-motor control problems may have difficulty controlling this saliva in the mouth, and may start to dribble or cough. If the child coughs or aspirates saliva, anxiety may be constantly associated with eating and drinking. This in turn may cause the child's tone to increase or become more unstable, and will make swallowing even more difficult.

The most important area to assess when a child is eating and drinking is the coordination between **swallowing, and breathing**. Many children with CP habitually breathe through their mouths, rather than through their noses. The pattern of breathing may be irregular due to the occurrence of spasms or involuntary movements. When food or drink is presented to the child, she is, therefore, at much greater risk of **aspiration** (food going into the airway) which can cause chest infections or pneumonia.

Symptoms of aspiration

When observing a child eating or drinking, it is important to assess what happens when he swallows. Many indications of aspiration can be heard, such as noisy breathing (the sound of needing to clear the throat), coughing, and prolonged apnoeas (when breathing stops). Other indications of aspiration may include blinking, blueness around the child's mouth, gagging/vomiting, and a look of fear/anxiety on the child's face. The child may make many attempts to initiate a swallow, and the swallow may only partially clear the oropharynx. In some children there is a delay in the triggering of the swallow reflex, by which time some of the food may already have fallen into the opening of the airway (a delayed swallow). Symptoms of aspiration may occur only when the child eats one particular texture. For example, many children are able to swallow soft, puréed foods safely, but when given water, which is more difficult to control, they may choke. All symptoms of aspiration are a serious cause for concern and indicate that therapy is needed for the child's safety and health. Intervention to minimise aspiration and thereby preserve the health of the child can be highly effective.

Oral sensory awareness

Oral sensory awareness is often disturbed in children who have abnormal postural tone, and this is an important area to evaluate. It is widely recognised that many children are *hypersensitive* to stimulation around and inside their mouths, but there are also many who are *hyposensitive* to oral stimulation. The two problems may superficially look similar. Both types of sensory disturbance may put the child at risk of aspiration when eating and drinking, and may worsen without intervention.

Hypersensitivity (oversensitivity)

The child has a stronger reaction to sensory stimulation than one would expect. The sensory threshold is lowered.

Hyposensitivity (undersensitivity)

The child shows a reduced reaction to sensory stimulation and does not respond quickly enough. The gag, cough and swallow reflexes are not as active as they should be. The sensory threshold is elevated.

The following signs and symptoms may suggest that a child has abnormal sensory awareness: crying, withdrawal from food or drink, grimacing, blinking, an increase in tone, increase in involuntary movements, occurrence of spasms, and vomiting. A child who is hypersensitive may also gag excessively, and be hypersensitive to touch in other parts of their body, such as his hands. The child who is hyposensitive will usually have an underactive gag reflex, a delayed or depressed swallow reflex, and a depressed or absent cough reflex. As a result of the underactivity of these protective reflexes, the hyposensitive child is at a great risk of aspiration and its related health problems.

Oral stage

Once the child has taken food into his mouth, there are some typical problems in dealing with the food that can be recognised:

Jaw

Where there is a marked increase in tone, the jaw is often seen to be restricted in movement. It may be retracted (pulled back) and may open only a limited amount. Where postural tone is moderately increased, and in cases of fluctuating tone, the jaw is often seen to open and close too much. It lacks the stability that is needed for it to open with graded movement and to provide a basis for controlled selective movements of the tongue, lips and cheeks. The opening and closing of the jaw is often rhythmical, and there are no lateral or rotatory movements that would enable the child to chew. In some cases, where children experience sharp increases in postural tone or 'spasms', the jaw is clenched tightly shut in a 'bite reflex'. This may be frightening and painful for the child as she is unable to release the bite. It is not uncommon for children to bite their own fingers or the inside of the mouth in this way.

Tongue

In cases of severe spasticity, the tongue may be lacking in movement and appear to be very 'bunched up' in the mouth. It may also be retracted. Where the increase in tone is more moderate, or where tone fluctuates, it is common to see the tongue moving only in a forward and backward pattern in a kind of modified sucking movement. This is usually in association with the opening and closing of the jaw. In cases where the child is quite extended, a 'tongue thrust' may be seen. A child may cause an open sore to develop on the underside of his tongue due to persistent rubbing over the lower central teeth. Little or no movement of the tongue to the sides of the mouth is seen, except in some cases of children with involuntary movements.

Lips

The lips may remain inactive during eating, allowing considerable spillage (see pre-oral stage). For this reason, it is common for children to be tipped back slightly in an attempt to keep food from falling or being pushed out of the mouth.

Throughout the oral stage, there is a risk of food being inhaled. It is important to listen to breathing sounds and to observe the child's facial expressions carefully. Any possible indications of aspiration should be noted and monitored carefully.

Swallowing

The eating and drinking patterns described above often result in there being little opportunity for food to be coated in saliva as a preparation for swallowing. When the child comes to swallow, food may therefore be inadequately prepared, and difficult to swallow. Many children need to swallow many times to clear their mouths due to the inefficient movements of the tongue and lips. Food may be pushed forwards out of the mouth through open lips, causing spillage.

In a child who is hyposensitive inside her mouth, food may reach the back of the mouth without triggering off the swallow reflex (the swallow is 'delayed'). There is then a great danger of food entering the airway, and causing coughing or choking. If the cough reflex is underactive, there may be 'silent aspiration'. This describes the situation where food goes into the airway without any obvious indication that this is happening.

Gastro-oesophageal reflux

According to some estimations, as many as 75 per cent of children with CP may suffer from the symptoms of gastro-oesophageal reflux (Rempel et al., 1988). This is the regurgitation of food upwards from the stomach into the oesophagus. In some cases food may come up only a little way, but in many cases refluxed food comes up to the opening of the airway where it can be aspirated or be vomitted out. Reflux may cause children to suffer chronic pain and malnourishment, and in severe cases it may cause fatal illness.

Reflux may be the main cause of loss of appetite, food refusal and ill health. This is because food coming up from the stomach is very acidic, and the high acidity may cause serious damage to the lining of the oesophagus (oesophagitis) and chronic pain associated with eating. Despite this damaging effect, the majority of cases of gastro-oesophageal reflux are unrecognised.

The child who suffers from this condition may appear to be hungry, but after a few mouthfuls becomes distressed and refuses to take more food. Turning away from food, arching the back and crying regularly at mealtimes is common. After mealtimes, the child may appear to regurgitate small amounts of food for a long time, and to suffer badly from 'wind'. Many children vomit after eating. If gastro-oesophageal reflux is recognised, there is much that can be done to alleviate the problem by managing the texture of food that the child is given, and the position used for eating and drinking. Management by medication, and in the most severe cases, by surgery, is becoming commonplace in some countries.

Communication at mealtimes

Assessment of mealtimes cannot be complete without an evaluation of the process of communication. From early infancy and throughout childhood, feeding times play an essential role in helping children to learn communication skills. In addition, good communication is essential for children to be able to eat in a safe and relaxed manner.

During a mealtime, it is important to observe the interaction between child and carer. How are likes and dislikes communicated? How does the carer know whether the child has had enough or wants more, or whether the eating process is causing discomfort? Many children with CP who have eating and drinking problems attempt to communicate such messages via *non-verbal* means. These may include facial expressions, eye movements, using voice, gestures or whole body movements. With a little practice, an observer can begin to identify what a child is attempting to communicate. For example, a child who is looking at a drink is probably indicating thirst and asking for a drink. A child who is becoming unstable and turning away from food is probably communicating that he doesn't want any more, or that he is in discomfort. Until such 'messages' are understood by the person assisting in the eating and drinking process, improvements in managing mealtimes and the safety of eating and drinking will be limited.

Management of eating and drinking difficulties

The therapist's priority in managing eating and drinking problems should be to make the process of eating and drinking as safe as possible. The health of the child is of paramount importance, and, therefore, prevention or minimising of aspiration and gastro-oesophageal reflux, in addition to provision of an adequate diet, should be immediate priorities. Most parents will be relieved to be able to describe their concerns about mealtimes and eating habits to a therapist. It is important to listen to these concerns and to work with the parent and child together to address them in practical ways.

The key to being able to effectively help children who have difficulty in eating and drinking is in understanding how the oral patterns arise from the child's overall patterns of movement. In all but the most severe cases, the ability to eat safely may be determined by the child's position at eating and drinking times. There is no benefit in changing the way in which children chew or drink for example, without first ensuring that their posture and alignment are optimal. Although no two children are exactly alike, principles of safe positioning for eating and drinking can be identified. These principles can be applied irrespective of whether a sitting or supported standing position is adopted for mealtimes.

General principles of positioning for eating and drinking

Stability

A good position for mealtimes requires the child to be well supported and in a stable position. Head and trunk stability are essential for safe eating. As food approaches, the child may become stiffer, or experience more involuntary movements, but the position should allow the child to remain as still as possible. The child must feel comfortable, secure and relaxed.

Alignment and symmetry

The ability to control the mouth for eating and drinking is dependant on the head and trunk being not only stable, but in good alignment. The body should be as symmetrical as possible, with the head in midline and the trunk well-aligned.

Elongation of the back of the neck

Regardless of whether we are eating in a sitting, standing, or reclining position, we always maintain elongation of the back of our necks when we are eating and drinking, and keep our chins tucked in. This is the most important aspect of positioning, and one which should not be compromised.

When the head is well forward, and the back of the neck elongated, we can provide the maximum protection for our airway to prevent food or liquid being aspirated. When we allow the head to tip back, there is always an increased risk of choking or food entering the airway. The spine should be straight. If the child's back is rounded in a sitting or standing position, the child will extend her neck, compromising the effective protection of her airway. If the feeder feels resistance to elongation of the back of the child's neck, then careful assessment of the spine will often reveal that it is flexed. In these cases, it is often helpful to allow the child to extend a little at the hips, which in turn will allow better extension of the spine and elongation of the back of the neck.

The majority of children with eating and drinking problems require assistance to achieve this position. It is therefore often helpful to use a handling technique known as *oral control* to keep the head and trunk stable, and maintain elongation of the back of the neck.

Comfort

Children should be comfortable and as relaxed as possible during eating and drinking. This is so that their tone remains as stable as possible and that their position is still. Anxiety about mealtimes often causes an increase in tone, involuntary movements or the occurrence of spasms, and this in turn makes the process of eating and drinking more difficult.

Some useful positions for mealtimes:

(*a*) The feeder can use her leg to help keep the child's spine straight, and by sinking the child's hips down a little, can minimise extensor spasms. Oral control may be provided as necessary.

(*b*) The feeder can keep the child's head position stable, and maintain face-to-face contact to facilitate communication.

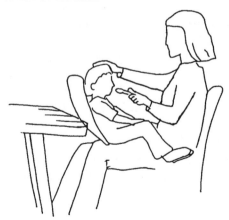

Position of the mealtime assistant

The position of the feeder in relation to the child who is eating has a significant effect on the child's own position, and, therefore, on eating patterns. Ideally the child should be able to look at the person who is feeding her, and this can be done in such a way as to encourage the optimum position of the head, keeping the back of the neck elongated and the chin tucked in. The child needs to be able to make eye contact with her feeder so that she can communicate her needs and feelings during mealtime, and also be able to watch food coming towards her.

Supporting the feet

Ideally, a child's feet should be supported on the floor or a footrest to increase his stability. There are some children, however, who will use their feet to push against a flat surface, and this will make them unstable. In these cases, it is better for the child's feet to be left unsupported.

Sitting on a low bench. The child is well supported by the feeder's legs, enabling one hand to provide oral control and the other to present food.

Sitting, standing or reclining?

Whichever position a child is placed in to eat, whether on the lap, in a chair or other piece of equipment, the above principles can be used as a guide. If a child is in a semi-reclining position on the lap for example, it remains essential to ensure that the back of the neck is elongated and the chin tucked in. In general, it is easier to maintain a good position whilst feeding a young child on the lap. This is because the feeder can adapt his or her position to give maximum support to the child.

Involving the child's hands

From the earliest stages in feeding babies and young children, it is important to involve their hands. Hands play a vital role in giving a child sensory input from which he can learn, and in enabling him to play an active part in controlling the eating and drinking process. A child as young as 4 months can use his hands to pull food towards his mouth or push it away. When feeding a child with CP, we can encourage him to place his hands around a bottle if one is used, and to feel the food with his fingers. It is often helpful to place a table or other flat surface in front of the child during mealtime to encourage active participation both in exploration of the food and in communicating needs. For some, attempts to hold a bottle or spoon, which involve the child grasping with his hand, will cause an increase in tone. When this is the case, the child may be able to hold the utensils before or after eating, or in a play situation, so that the eating and drinking process is not compromised by increasing tone or involuntary movements.

Oral control

The most important aspect of a child's position is the relationship between the head and trunk. Head control, and the ability to use the jaw as a stable basis from which the tongue, lips and cheeks can work, is a vital prerequisite for mature swallowing, chewing and drinking. Many children with CP have great difficulty maintaining a stable head position themselves, and as a result they often have ungraded movements of the jaw.

When a child has poor head control or difficulty controlling his jaw movements, 'oral control' may be provided by the person assisting. The mealtime assistant uses his or her arm and hand to maintain a good head position, and to help the child move the jaw in a more controlled and graded way.

The assistant's arm is placed around the back of the child's neck. The upper part of the arm or inside of the elbow is used to maintain elongation of the back of the neck. The middle finger is placed under the chin, just behind the bone, and applies firm pressure to keep the jaw stable. As the child opens his mouth, the finger maintains constant pressure, allowing just sufficient opening for the food to be placed in the child's mouth, and then helping the child to maintain a closed mouth during swallowing.

The index finger is usually placed on the front of the child's chin just below the lip. This helps to keep the head position stable, and to counter the upwards pressure from the middle finger under the chin (thus ensuring that the head is not tipped upwards). When the jaw is stable, the lower lip will usually be able to function well, but in cases where it does not, the feeder's index finger can be used to facilitate its movement.

The feeder's thumb rests on the child's face near the ear, or is held right away from the face. Its role is mainly to help the feeder keep his or her hand in a stable position, although it may sometimes help to prevent the jaw from deviating to one side or another. Occasionally, the thumb may interfere with the eating process due to a retained rooting reflex which causes the child to turn towards it. In these cases, it will help to make sure there is no contact between the thumb and the side of the face.

It may take a while for some children to feel comfortable with oral control. For most children it is best to introduce it at a snacktime rather than at a main meal. The handling should be firm and consistent so that the child does not feel the hand moving around. It may be helpful to apply oral control at first with the thumb only, stabilising the jaw from below, with the rest of the fingers placed on the sternum (Illustration c). The sternum will then be used as a key point of control, and can help to prevent the child from pushing back into extension.

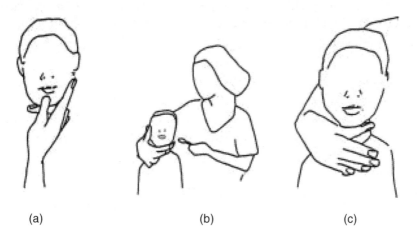

(a) (b) (c)

Oral control:

(a) From the front.
(b) From the side.
(c) From the side, using the sternum as key point of control.

Spoon feeding

Use oral control to keep the head in a good position and to maintain stability of the jaw. Ideally, the spoon should have a flat bowl, enabling the child to feel the food on her lips when they close, and to effectively remove it. It may be helpful to use a durable plastic spoon so that the child is not afraid of biting on hard metal.

Food presented by spoon should be of a uniform mashed consistency. Try to avoid very runny textures or food containing hard lumps on a spoon. If the food is hard enough to need chewing, it is better to give it by hand as described below.

Always present the spoon in the midline, and place it flat on the front of the tongue. Provision of oral control enables the jaw to open just enough to allow the spoon into the mouth. Apply firm pressure downwards on the front of the tongue, and then wait for the child to begin to lower her top lip. As she does so, you may assist by closing the lower jaw, and removing the spoon. This is done in one smooth movement, so that there is only one opening and closure of the jaw, and the child does not have the opportunity to bite up and down on the spoon. Maintain oral closure until that mouthful has been completely swallowed and you have heard a clear breath. You can then proceed with the next spoonful.

The application of firm pressure downwards on the front of the tongue helps to bring the tongue to a normal starting point from which to swallow, and to minimise tongue-thrusting. Make sure that the spoon does not press backwards on the tongue, since this may cause the child to gag. The downwards pressure from the spoon also facilitates lip closure, and enables the child to remove food from the spoon without it being scraped off against the top teeth.

Developing chewing

In order to develop chewing, it is necessary to present food by hand or finger. Select pieces of food that are easy to chew to begin with. Food that dissolves or becomes very soft when it is first chewed is ideal. Certain types of snack foods such 'Quavers' and 'Wotsits' dissolve once they have been bitten, and can then be safely swallowed without fear of pieces causing choking. Pieces of toast may also be suitable, or French fries.

Place a piece of 'bite-and-dissolve' food between the child's teeth on the side of the mouth and hold it there. Use oral control to ensure that the head is kept in a good position, and that the mouth opens and closes with graded movement. The child may bite on the food straightaway, but if he does not, then move the food lightly to stimulate biting. As the child opens and closes his jaw to chew, it is usually possible to see that lateral movement of the tongue is also stimulated. Keep holding the food at the side of the child's mouth until it is softened and then sucked on to the tongue. It will then be further sucked and then swallowed. Use oral control throughout to ensure lip closure during swallowing, and to maintain graded jaw movements.

The role of the oral control is to limit jaw-opening. It is not to move the jaw in a chewing pattern. The child will move his jaw himself, and the hand providing oral control will act as a limiter, to keep this movement in a more normal range.

As the child becomes accustomed to chewing foods that dissolve easily, progress on to foods that are more chewable: bread, cooked vegetables, ripe fruit etc., all of which can be given by being placed to the sides of the mouth. Avoid hard textures such as raw carrot and apple which may be dangerous and cause choking. Try to finger-feed some food at each mealtime. Some children may take food more easily in this way than from a spoon. It is also important for the child to be able to feel the texture of the food in his hands. Ideally, every texture should be introduced to the hands prior to being placed in the mouth, although the child may not be able to hold the food and eat at the same time.

For many children with CP, food that needs to be chewed will always need to be presented in this way. Some will be able to progress to being able to move food to the sides of their mouths themselves, and then may be able to finger-feed themselves. Those children who have very poor head and jaw control may benefit from practising chewing in safety by being given the opportunity to chew on some dried fruit wrapped in a pouch made of a cotton handkerchief or piece of muslin. In this way, the child can taste the dried fruit and practise the movements of chewing without there being danger of choking. The pouch is held at all times by the feeder.

Drinking

To develop a safe drinking pattern, good positioning and use of oral control is very important. Many children find it difficult to control thin, runny fluids in their mouths and are, therefore, in danger of frequent choking during drinking. For this reason it is often best to introduce drinking with liquids that are naturally thick, such as puréed fruit, yoghurt, custard, or drinks thickened with a thickening agent. Thick fluids move slowly and are relatively heavy, thereby giving increased sensory information to the mouth. Introduce the thickened liquids in an open cup. A soft plastic cup with a 'cut-out' may be useful so that the child does not need to tip his head back as the cup is tipped up. A doidy cup (which slopes to one side) is another suitable alternative which enables the cup to be tipped whilst the child's head stays upright.

Use oral control. Tip the cup before presenting it to the child so that the fluid is already at the rim. Place the cup on the lower lip in front of the teeth. Tip so that the liquid just reaches the lips, and wait for the child to move his top lip. The child will be able to feel the liquid on his lips since the mouth is only slightly open.

Young children often learn to drink from a cup with a spout. This is not appropriate for children with CP since use of a spout reinforces an immature sucking pattern, and may cause exaggerated tongue thrusting to develop.

Once the child has got used to taking a few sips in this way, try to establish a rhythm of drinking. In this way, he can anticipate that he will take three sips, for example, and then the cup will be removed for him to close his lips to swallow and then breathe comfortably. It may be helpful to count aloud—'one, two, three, rest....'

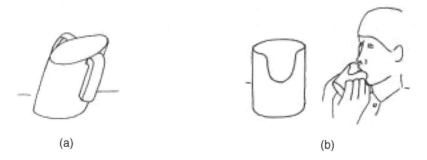

(a)   (b)

(a) Doidy cup.
(b) A cup with a small piece cut out to enable it to be tipped without the child's neck extending.

Some specific problems

Managing problems of sensation

On the basis of an initial assessment, it is often difficult to evaluate the nature and extent of sensory problems. The superficial symptoms of hypersensitivity and hyposensitivity may appear similar; in both cases the child may dislike eating and drinking, and may turn away from food. In many cases, children who are hyposensitive inside their mouths may also be hypersensitive on the face and around the mouth in particular.

In management of children with sensory problems, the priority is to ensure that the child has adequate protection of the airway during eating and drinking. Through careful manipulation of the child's position, the texture of food and fluids, and use of feeding techniques, it is usually possible to bring about a significant change in eating patterns and to minimise health risks. Management comprises a combination of grading the sensory stimulation of eating so that the child can swallow most effectively, and through use of handling techniques and good positioning, enabling the child to grade her motor responses during eating.

The child who is hypersensitive will benefit from therapeutic input away from mealtimes. Introduce the child to things such as a toothbrush, a rattle, or a spoon which can be safely explored by putting them in the mouth. Encourage the child to enjoy exploring a variety of textures in this way. Young children enjoy playing with their own fingers inside their mouths, and may gradually get used to playing with a small toothbrush or soft rubber toy.

By progressing in very small steps, expect the child to tolerate exploring things in the mouth for slightly longer periods, and introduce a few different textures. When the child expresses slight anxiety or discomfort with the toy, keep still and wait for the child to adjust to the stimulation and relax. It is important not to push the child beyond what can be comfortably tolerated—if the experience becomes unpleasant or over-stimulating, then increasing hypersensitivity and hypertonicity will result, rather than assisting the child to tolerate stimulation at a more normal level. Remember that the goal of this process is to enable the child to cope better with a variety of textures of food, and to be able to eat and drink more safely.

The child who is hyposensitive can often respond more effectively to the stimulation of food and drink in her mouth when given adequate time. Good positioning and oral control is essential to ensure protection of the airway. Careful spoon-feeding of food of a cohesive mashed texture, with firm pressure applied on to the tongue to facilitate good tongue movement, can often stimulate a safe swallow. Food that is cold or has a strong flavour (spicy foods) may be easier for the child to eat. When given ample time and adequate stimulation, depressed reflexes can improve. Always ensure a child has time to clear each mouthful and inhale comfortably between each mouthful. Runny fluid may be easily aspirated in the hyposensitive child, and is often best substituted by thickened liquids.

Tongue thrust

A tongue thrust is a forward/backward sucking movement which may be exaggerated by increased tone. It is part of an extensor pattern and is indicative of a lack of jaw stability. The child with a tongue thrust usually has little or no spontaneous lateral movements of the tongue, or chewing.

A tongue thrust can usually be modified or minimised by careful positioning and use of oral control. The use of a good spoon-feeding technique is another effective way of reducing tongue thrust and facilitating more normal tongue movement patterns. Presentation of runny food on a spoon often exaggerates tongue thrusting and, therefore, should be avoided. Food of a more cohesive mashed texture is suitable for spoon-feeding. It is also beneficial to work towards developing chewing, and thereby a more normal range of tongue movements, and drinking with provision of oral control aimed towards controlling fluid intake from an open cup.

Tonic bite reflex

This is an often distressing pattern of biting that occurs without voluntary control by the child. It involves sustained biting together of the jaws and is usually triggered by touch, especially to the front teeth. The tonic bite reflex is almost always part of a generalised flexor spasm and should not be seen as something that involves the mouth in isolation. It is usually indicative of some degree of hypersensitivity, and occurs in children whose tone can rise sharply to quite high levels of spasticity. A child with a bite reflex may also grind her teeth and accidentally bite her own cheeks, tongue or fingers.

Reducing hypersensitivity is a vital part of helping a child to overcome a bite reflex. Play which involves the child handling a variety of textures and getting used to releasing grasp is important. Positioning to minimise the occurrence of flexor spasms should be considered; children with bite reflexes may be able to eat and drink with less disturbance from spasms in a prone standing frame, with the provision of good oral control. Development of chewing will lead to a more normal variety of movement patterns of the jaw and tongue, and chewing at the beginning of a meal may help to relax the jaw. Spoon-feeding is often difficult in children with strong bite reflexes, but use of a good technique which will at first trigger the bite reflex to occur, can be very effective in diminishing the occurrence of the bite. Children who have strong bite reflexes often associate eating and drinking with pain and fear. It is important for the mealtime assistant to remain calm when the bite reflex occurs, to encourage the child to remain as relaxed as possible, and to wait for the spasm to pass.

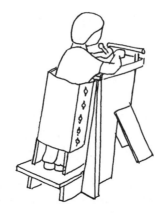

Child in prone standing frame. This position is often helpful for children who
have tonic bite reflexes or who suffer from gastro-oesophageal reflux.

Gastro-oesophageal reflux

Children who suffer from the effects of gastro-oesophageal reflux can be helped by careful
positioning during and after mealtimes, controlling the texture of food, and the timing
of mealtimes and snacks. Gastro-oesophageal reflux may be caused by an increase in
abdominal pressure, and for many children, this can be minimised by careful positioning.
Positioning in a prone standing frame, for example, will minimise the effects of flexor
spasms and keep the child in a position where gravity helps the passage of food through
the digestive system, and in particular, through the stomach. Many children will be

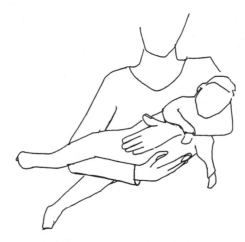

Carrying position for minimising flexor spasms and relief of discomfort associated
with gastro-oesophageal reflux. Gravity aids gastric emptying and abdominal
pressure is kept as stable as possible.

helped by remaining in an upright position after eating for up to half an hour or longer, if possible. For a child who cannot be stood in this way, discomfort associated with gastro-oesophageal reflux may be relieved by holding her in an extended position, whilst keeping her head elevated as shown. Gastric emptying is aided in this position and flexor spasms may be minimised. Child may also benefit from sleeping with her mattress tilted up to 30 degrees, so that gravity aids the passage of food through the digestive system.

A child may be less prone to gastro-oesophageal reflux if she does not eat large quantities of food at any one time. The occurrence of reflux may be reduced by offering 4 or 5 small meals each day, rather than 3 large ones. In this way, the stomach does not become so full and distended, and gastro-oesophageal reflux is less likely to occur.

Introduction of thick liquids for drinking may be of benefit since food of a thicker texture is less likely to be refluxed than runny liquids. From 4 months old, children can be introduced to solid food. In many cases, a reduction in the incidence of vomiting and reflux may occur at this stage.

Children who suffer from oesophagitis often find acidic foods such as fruit, painful to swallow. Avoidance of very acidic food may help to maintain an adequate diet in children who may otherwise refuse to eat.

The importance of oral hygiene

Children with CP are particularly susceptible to dental caries and gum disease which could lead to discomfort in the mouth and exacerbation of eating and drinking problems. This is due in part to limited selective tongue movements which normally help to keep teeth clean, lack of saliva due to dribbling, hypersensitivity and diets which may be high in sugar to increase calorie intake. Good dental hygiene can be introduced from a very young age to minimise the occurrence of dental health problems. This entails provision of healthy oral stimulation which can help to increase tolerance of food textures and lay a good foundation for development of chewing and saliva control.

Gum massage

Even before an infant's first teeth have erupted, regular gum massage can be provided. It is important that the child is comfortable for this, and that he is positioned with his head upright, chin tucked in and back of neck elongated. For many children, the provision of oral control is necessary to maintain such a stable position, as in eating and drinking.

Gum massage should be pleasurable for a child, and if gagging is caused, or the child shows any sign of distress, it should be stopped. It is always possible to find a level of stimulation (although this may be very little indeed for some children) where the child is comfortable, and not distressed. When this level has been found, the carer should be able to progress in tiny steps, to enable the child to comfortably tolerate a little more stimulation to his face or mouth. It is helpful to remember that firm, steady pressure is always more easily tolerated than light touch, and that all movements should be slow so that the child is able to adapt to every movement he feels and remain relaxed.

The carer may start by rolling a wet finger inside the child's top lip, slightly to one side. Gradually rub the finger steadily along the line of the upper jaw on one side, back and forward a couple of times. Remove the finger to give the child a chance to swallow and remain relaxed, then proceed with the next 'quarter' of the mouth. Finally, massage along the child's lower gums in the same way. During this process, oral control will be necessary for a majority of children to ensure that the head is kept stable and that the child does not gag. Oral control will also enable the carer to keep the mouth as closed as possible during this process. It may be advisable to wear protective rubber gloves for this procedure to minimise the possibility of transfer of infection between the carer and child.

Toothbrushing

Once the child starts to develop teeth, this process can be carried out with a small toothbrush. If a baby's rubber toothbrush is available, many young children will enjoy munching on this. It may also provide good practice for developing chewing skills. If the child finds it too difficult to tolerate a toothbrush, then it is preferable to continue tooth-cleaning with a finger, and with the possible introduction of a small amount of toothpaste.

The toothbrush is used in a pattern similar to the finger in gum massage. Oral control is usually necessary to ensure that the child's head is held in a stable, upright position, maintaining elongation of the back of the neck. Treat the mouth in four sections. When brushing the upper jaw, brush the teeth from top to bottom, and from the back of the mouth to the front. When brushing the lower jaw, brush the teeth bottom to top, and again, from the back of the mouth to the front. After each section, remove the brush, allowing the child enough time to spit out any excess water or toothpaste, and to do several relaxed breaths before beginning the next section. Toothbrushing is a very stimulatory activity, and most children will need time to get used to it. It should not cause gagging, and if it appears to be doing so, then it is wise to use a finger instead of the brush for a while.

Nutritional issues

Many children with eating and drinking difficulties do not receive an adequate or balanced diet. It is common for children with CP to suffer from constipation, and to be both short and underweight for their age.

To some extent, poor weight gain may be minimised by providing as many calories as possible in the texture that the child can eat the most efficiently. For example, some children are able to drink thickened liquids from a cup more easily than taking solid foods in other forms. In these cases, it would be beneficial to provide as many calories in a liquid texture as possible.

Poor fluid intake often contributes to the tendency of many children with CP to be constipated. Increasing fluid intake often requires development of drinking skills as outlined earlier, and the introduction of drinking thickened liquids. It is particularly important to try to increase the amount of water intake in cases of constipation.

Looking after a child with eating and drinking difficulties may cause considerable stress and anxiety to carers. In many instances, carers spend excessive amounts of time trying to give sufficient food to the children in their care. It may often be found that after 30–40 minutes of eating and drinking, children become so fatigued that beyond this time negligible amounts of food are consumed. For many children, it is advisable to take a rest from the mealtime at this point, and to consider introducing an additional snack to the daily routine to provide further nutrition. In this way, an overall reduction in the amount of feeding time can be made, without reducing the quantity of food or fluid that is consumed.

References

Bax, M. 'Eating is important', Editorial, *Developmental Medicine and Child Neurology* 31(1989): 285–86.

Gisel, E.G., Applegate-Ferrante, T., Benson, J. and **Bosma, J.F.** 'Oral-motor skills following sensorimotor therapy in two groups of moderately dysphagic children with cerebral palsy: aspiration vs nonaspiration', *Dysphagia* 11(1996): 59–71.

Gisel, E.G. and **Patrick, J.** 'Identification of children with cerebral palsy, unable to maintain a normal nutritional state', *Lancet* 1(1988): 283–86.

Humphrey, T. 'Reflex activity in the oral and facial area of the human fetus'. In Bosma, J.F. (ed.), second symposium on oral sensation and perception, Springfield, IL: Thomas, 1970: 195–233.

Larnert, G. and **Ekberg, O.** 'Positioning improves the oral and pharyngeal swallowing function in children with cerebral palsy', *Acta Paediatrica* 84(1995): 689–92.

Rempel, G.R., Colwell S.O. and **Nelson, R.P.** 'Growth in children with cerebral palsy fed via gastrostomy', *Paediatrics* 82(1988): 857–62.

Marian Browne graduated from Sheffield University in 1986 with a Bachelor of Medical Science in Speech Science. She has been working as Speech and Language Therapy Tutor at the Bobath Centre for Children with Cerebral Palsy, London for 11 years. She has also worked in the field of paediatrics in Cambridge and in London. She has particular interest in the management of eating and drinking difficulties and is involved in the postgraduate training of therapists in this field.

Appendix A

How to make equipment from appropriate paper-based technology (APT)

Jean Westmacott

Appropriate Paper-based Technology (APT) is a cost-effective way to produce personally designed furniture or other objects for use and creativity from recycled paper and cardboard.

Materials	• Paper
	• Thin card, for example, from shoeboxes
	• Corrugated cardboard
	• Soft string or recycled tights for internal ties
	• Flour for making paste
Tools	• Knives—strong blade for cutting straight edges, thin blade with sharp point for cutting holes
	• Kettle or means of boiling water to make paste
	• Bowl or jug and large spoon for making paste

Materials are waste paper, card and corrugated cardboard boxes. Flour is used for paste, and varnish or waterproof paint is used to seal the completed items. All that is needed by way of tools are a kettle or pan to boil water, a suitable receptacle to make the paste, knives and a smooth stick. Once the techniques are mastered, endless variations of equipment can be made, and a workshop is not necessary. It is quite easy to make APT items at home, outdoors in dry countries, or in any community room.

Using weak materials to make strong equipment

Paper and card are essentially weak materials; it is the design of the structure and the quality of workmanship that brings the strength. The best tip for keeping the design strong is to keep in mind the forces of **pressure** and **tension**.

• Pressure is exerted on weight-bearing surface when the item is in use. It could make the surface break, bend or dent. To prevent this, layers of cardboard and paper are used; the heavier the person, the more the layers.

- Tension is the pulling force exerted on joints, axles or handles when the equipment is in use. Rods, thin card 'angle-irons', ties and straps of layered paper are used to strengthen joints against the force of tension. The neater and firmer the strapping of the joints, the stronger they are

To make a stool or small bench

This incorporates a lot of the techniques needed for other equipment and is a good starting point for making APT items. First decide on the length and width of the top of the stool and then the height (this will depend on the child and the use).

Pieces for stool

1. Mark out the top on a flat piece of corrugated cardboard, making sure each corner is 90 degrees (check angle by using the corner of a book).
2. Cut it out with a sharp knife using a ruler or a piece of card to keep the cutting line straight.

N.B. When cutting, hold knife so that it's blade is at 90 degrees to cardboard so the top and bottom edges stay equal.

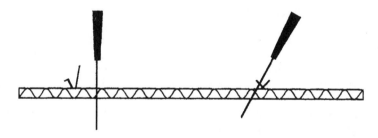

3. Use the first board cut for each piece as a template to cut more pieces exactly the same size. The number of pieces depends on the cardboard and the size of the person using the stool—have enough so that the thickness of them stacked together comes to 2 cm. The pieces will be stronger if the corrugations run across the width and across the length in alternate layers.

Alternate layering for boards

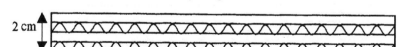

Corrugations in alternate directions.

4. The legs are easily made from two boards of the same width as the stool top. Their length will be the height you require, minus 2 cm (or the thickness of the stool top).

5. A central 'leg' or spacer to run at right angles to the end legs, is needed. Cut it the same height as the end legs. The length will be the length of the top minus the thickness of the two end legs.

6. Make paste. Take 2 dessert spoonfuls of flour made from wheat, finely-ground maize or cassava, or maida, and mix with about 100 ml of cold water until the mixture is free of lumps and looks like smooth cream. Quickly add about 400 ml of boiling water, stirring continuously.

Making paste

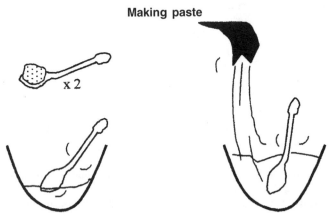

Mix 2 dessert spoonfuls of flour with cold water—it should look like thick cream.

Pour in water that is still boiling. Do this rapidly while stirring. Pour in to make about 500 ml.

N.B. Water must still be at boiling point. The paste should feel sticky.

7. Cut the pieces for the end and central legs in the same way as the pieces for the top, and paste together the layers for each piece. Paste the layers together by applying a thin layer of paste on each side of the boards where they will attach to each other. Put the pieces together and press flat while they dry. Place some sheets of dry newspaper under the layered pieces with some more dry newspaper on top.

   Finally, place a flat board or table upside-down on this, making sure it covers the whole piece. If necessary, put some weight like some books on top.

Pressing

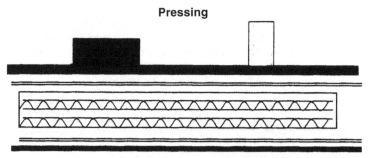

Dry sheets of newspaper on each side of boards being pressed flat, lying under a flat wooden board.

8. N.B. Check and air the layered piece and change the newspaper every day until flat and dry.

9. When the pieces are dry, roll rods from thin cards. You will need one rod every 15 cm to support the top. Make the rods by applying paste on a piece of thin card that is about 8 cm longer than the width of the stool. Make this into a rod by rolling it around a broomstick or similar smooth stick. Pull it off the stick and rub to make sure the edges stay stuck. If the edges are threatening to pull away, make a small strap to hold them down.

Rolling card into a rod

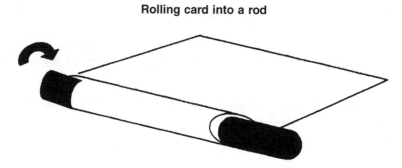

Roll tightly so there are no air gaps—the tighter the roll, the stronger the rod.

10. These rods will be placed directly under the stool top, across the width and through the top of each side leg. Circular holes, the same size as the ends of the rods, will have to be cut out of the top edges of the sides so that the top can rest on the rods. Cut these together so the holes are at the same place on each side.

11. Place stool pieces together to check all is correct. Check that the edges sit together neatly and that the top is level. Sometimes, sides need to be trimmed to ensure they are the same as each other, and that top and bottom are parallel.

Fitting support rod/s

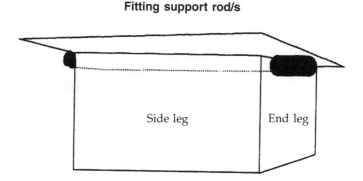

Side leg   End leg

12. Now everything needs to be attached together by starting with the joints.

'Angle-Irons' using thin card

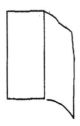 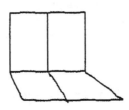 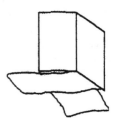

Fold piece of card in half. Fold again at right angles.

Tear lower portion in halves
along the line and cross over.

13. Apply some paste thinly all over 'angle-iron' and place firmly in the corner in the inside so that the top connects to two sides as in drawing.
14. Make straps of layered paper. (Newspaper works very well.) Make sure each piece of paper is placed with the grain in the same direction, so the layers making the straps will tear off together. Each strap should only be about 3 cm wide. (When covering edges that are curved, this should be far narrower.)

Connecting sides and top

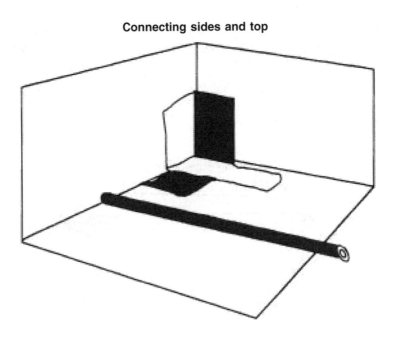

N.B. Rub well, so there are no air gaps.

Making straps

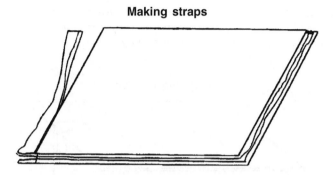

Always tear! It is quicker and it sticks better than if it is cut.

Apply paste thinly over a piece of newspaper. Place another piece the same size on top making sure the grain of the paper is running in the same direction. Add at least 4 layers of paper so that when you tear off a narrow strap of layered paper, it will be strong enough not to break when you pull it holding on to each end of the strap.

15. While working on the 'angle-irons' and straps inside the box, it helps to have a piece of string tied right around the outside of the box to hold the sides together temporarily. Once the inner joints are securely strapped, it can be removed before strapping the outside.
16. Check it is all rubbed down well with no small pieces lifting up or air bubbles trapped between layers.
17. Then strap the edges.

Strapping joints

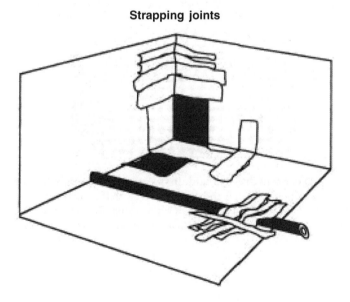

Overlap straps and place some 'fixing straps' too, at right angles to the other straps.
Joints are the places where furniture often starts to break, therefore, they need special attention.

18. When the joints are strapped inside, the stool can be turned over for strapping the outside.
19. When the joints and edges are completely strapped, the remaining flat parts can be filled more quickly. Use mosaics of paper, each one torn no larger than 7 cm by 7 cm so that they do not wrinkle.

Strapping outside

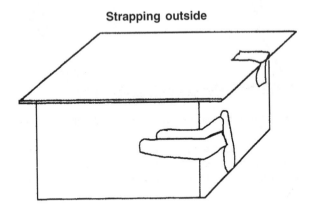

Rub flat—paste and pressure.

20. Then there is the fun of adding a decorative finish. This can be another single layer of gift paper, brown paper or a collage of pictures from magazines.

Decorative finish

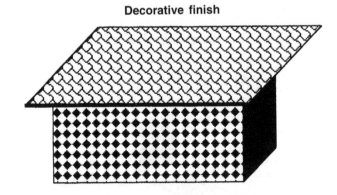

21. Leave until it is 100 per cent dry and hard. In dry weather, this only takes a week. Keep turning so the inside can be open to the air for drying as well as the outside.
22. Once dry, clear varnish can be used to give a professional finish and make it splash-proof. Gloss paint made for wood can also be used. (It will block out the newspaper print.)

Standing frame pattern

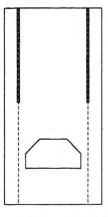

Prepare 2 side-pieces

o   Holes at top for rods.

---- Lines show position for prone support board and for upright strengthening board.

=   Lines show where slot will be cut when boards are dry and ready to assemble.

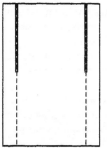

Prone support board

---- Lines show position for prone support board and for upright strengthening board.

=   Lines show where slot will be cut when boards are dry and ready to assemble.

⌒ Hole cut for footrest.

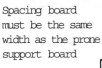

Spacing board

Smaller 'spacing' board to hold side pieces parallel in front.

=   Lines show where the slot will be cut (half-way) so that the upright strengthening board will slot into the 2 sides.

Spacing board must be the same width as the prone support board

Footrest

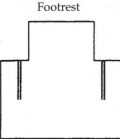

Tray

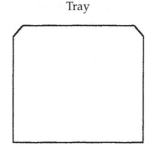

Standing frame

Knobs for fixing wide pelvic band (pelvic band not shown). Sew the band on the opposite side. On the knob side of the band, make holes to put over knobs.

Jean Westmacott runs People Potential, a training organisation with the aim of assisting individuals and organisations to develop and use their potential in practical work through research, knowledge and training. The specialist areas of work are in Appropriate Paper-based Technology, assistive furniture, educational toys and creative crafts. Training courses are run in the UK and world-wide.

She was funded by UK, Overseas Development Agency in 1988 to be trained in Appropriate Paper-based Technology by Bevill Packer, Zimbabwe. Since then she has researched the methods and worked on the safety and design of APT furniture and trained extensively in the methods.

Along with running courses through People Potential, she is also involved as Honorary Tutor at the Centre of International Child Health, UCL, London; and Advisor for the Consortium of organisations working on the Transfer of Innovative Methods, an EU project. She also provides training for Voluntary Service Overseas. See website on APT: www.apbt.org.uk.

Appendix B

Choosing appropriate play activities to engage a child's active involvement in therapy

Children need opportunities to play in order to learn. Young children play and learn in all their waking moments and, if we want to engage with them, we must understand the nature and purpose of their games.

At different stages in their development, children enjoy different play activities. The following table may help you to choose activities that the child you are working with is likely to enjoy.

Age	Activity
0–3 months	Enjoys making eye contact with familiar people. Later smiles in response to eye contact and smile from familiar person.
3–5 months	Enjoys being talked to. Enjoys songs. Likes to look at toys hanging within hands' reach. Enjoys having toys placed in his hands. Learns to bat a toy with his hands. When placed prone, he enjoys the sensation of scratching the floor with his fingers.
6–11 months	Laughs at peek-a-boo games. Likes to look at himself in a mirror. Recognises family members and knows their names if repeated often enough knows his own name. Manipulates all kinds of objects in his hands—brings everything to his mouth. Likes squeaky toys and rattles. Loves to be handled, carried about, bounced on his mother's lap or pushed along in a pushchair.
12 months	Enjoys hearing songs and nursery rhymes over and over again. Uses hands bilaterally: he can hold cup in one hand and drop object into it with the other, or he can hold a large, light ball with two hands. Enjoys finding things that have been hidden. Enjoys picking up tiny things between his finger and thumb. Likes toys that he can pull and push along.
18 months	Imitates all kinds of sounds and actions. Loves to listen to his mother telling him what she is doing as she goes about her chores. Loves to fetch and carry familiar objects when asked.

(Contd.)

(Contd.)

Age	Activity
	Enjoys putting things in containers and taking them out again.
	Likes to point to a few parts of his body that he knows.
	Enjoys looking at pictures of familiar objects.
2 years	Likes climbing, swinging and sliding.
	Loves simple stories.
3 years	Enjoys playing with other children.
	Begins to enjoy pretending—pretends to drive the car or sweep the floor, for example.
	Loves to push himself about on a tricycle or pedal car.
	Loves stories with pictures.

For a child with CP who will find it difficult to do all these things for himself in a normal way, it is important for those working with him to help him so that he will gain some of the experiences that will later help him make sense of the world around him. For instance, it is important for a child to learn to reach out for toys and bat them with outstretched fingers before he learns to grasp and bring things to his mouth. It is important for a child to learn to hold a toy in two hands so that he can later learn to coordinate using his hands together. He can be helped to do these things by hand-over-hand assistance from those working with him. The experience will help him to try the activity by himself later.

It is often tempting to give children toys that they will want to grasp and perhaps bring to their mouths. But this may lead to flexion and will spoil the active extension we are trying to encourage. It is worthwhile planning what toys are needed before starting work with a child. For example, if you could arrange for a ball to be suspended on a string just above where the child will be lying in prone, he will be interested straight away to reach up and push the ball away. He will then hold his head up to see the ball swing back.

A child of two years or so who enjoys putting objects into a container will reach up with rotation to where you are holding a small block. He can then bend down and drop in into a container which you have placed near his opposite knee. All the better if the container is a tin so that the brick will make a satisfying noise when it is dropped in.

Another variation on this game is to prop a plank with raised edges on a chair. The child uses two hands to lift an inflatable ball on to the higher end of the plank and watches it roll down to knock over the light plastic bottle you have placed in its path. This is a very useful game for a child to play while you are trying to facilitate active extension of his hips and knees. You may need to ask his mother to fetch the ball and replace the bottle each time, but you will be amazed how many times the child will carry on playing this game. This is because the activity gives him the opportunity to practise and discover how things can be made to happen, and this is appropriate for his present level of play.

Many times, working with athetoid children, we want them to hold postures rather than to move. In this case, it is important to find interesting things for the child to watch. Perhaps, you want the child to hold his trunk steady in standing while you facilitate extension in his knees and weight bearing on straight arms. You could try getting his mother to read him an interesting story, or you could get her to play peek-a-boo, or maybe he could watch another child rolling the ball down the plank.

Action songs done as a group are very interesting and exciting for children between 3 and 5 years. It is worthwhile trying to arrange for several children of similar age and conditions to come for treatment together.

Glossary

Abduction	Movement of a limb to the side away from the body.
Agonist	Muscle or groups of muscles that carry out the primary action in a movement. For example, the elbow flexors are the agonists when the elbow is flexed against gravity.
Adduction	Sideways movement of a limb from abduction back to the body or across the body.
Alignment	Three or more parts in a straight line.
Antagonist	Muscle or group of muscles that play out in a coordinated way to allow the agonists to carry out a smooth movement. For example, the elbow extensors are the antagonists when the elbow is flexed against gravity.
Anterior	In front of.
Associated movement	Coordinated movements occurring in the *absence* of spasticity. They are seen during early childhood where movements are more in total patterns. They are also seen throughout life when new motor skills are being learnt or where there is effort. Examples include mirror movements and facial grimacing.
Associated reaction	Abnormal increase in tone in one part of the body as a result of effort in another which is less affected. The reaction is associated with spasticity, and is seen as a movement in a child with mild to moderate spasticity and felt as an increase in tone in child with severe spasticity.
Asymmetric	One side of the body acts in a different way to the other.
Ataxic-Ataxia	Difficulty in coordinating movement, poor balance, clumsy, awkward voluntary movements.
Athetoid-Athetosis	From a Greek word meaning 'of no fixed posture'. Children with athetoid CP have no fixed posture because of involuntary movements and lack of coordinated co-contraction.
Balance	Ability to stay in and regain a position when the influence of gravity would otherwise cause a fall. This ability is the result of the interaction of righting, equilibrium and protective reactions.

Breaking up patterns	Changing one or two elements of the stereotyped patterns of movement that children with spasticity try to use to function. For example, the stereotyped pattern of extension in the lower limb is adduction, inward rotation and some flexion at the hip, extension in the knee and plantarflexion at the ankle. The pattern could be broken up (and be made more functional) by introducing either dorsiflexion at the ankle or extension in the hip (or both).
Calcaneous	Heel bone
Central nervous system	The brain and spinal cord.
Co-contraction	Normal co-contraction is the simultaneous activation of agonist and antagonist to give mobility with stability. It provides us with normal postural tone and allows smooth, graded coordinated movement.
Contraction	Normal activity in a muscle that causes it to shorten and bring about movement in a joint.
Contracture	Permanent shortening of a muscle, muscle tendon or joint structure. Once a contracture becomes established, fibrous tissue is laid down and then it can only be lengthened by surgery.
Coordination	Smooth efficient movement caused by the activity of muscles working together and controlled by the nervous system.
Creeping	Moving around the floor in prone on elbows. Legs are mostly inactive.
Crawling	Moving around the floor on hands and knees.
Deformity	Abnormal body posture or limb position. It can be fixed or unfixed.
Dissociation	Ability to move one body part and keep the rest still or to move one limb in one direction while another moves in the opposite direction, e.g., in crawling.
Diplegia	Whole body affected by CP but lower limbs more than upper limbs.
Distal	Situated away from central part of body.
Dorsiflexion	Movement at ankle joint that brings heel down and toes up; standing on the heels.
Equilibrium	State of balance.
Equilibrium reactions	Automatic and highly complex movements which serve to maintain and regain balance before, during and after displacement of the centre of gravity.

Eversion	Refers to the foot. The foot is everted when the sole is lifted from the ground and turned outwards to face away from the other foot while the person is standing.
Extension	To extend means to stretch out or make longer. Extension in the body means the limbs are straight, the trunk is upright or stretched out, and the head is up or pushed back.
Extensor tone	The state of tension in those muscles that extend the body.
Facilitation	A handling technique to make active movement easier; or to make active movement possible where it was not possible before.
Flexion	The opposite of extension. The limbs are bent up and the trunk is curved forward. In full flexion, the body and limbs would be curled up into a ball.
Flexor tone	The state of tension in those muscles that flex the body and limbs.
Function	Purposeful activity; useful motor abilities such as being able to hold one's head erect.
Gastro-oesophageal Reflux	Food coming up from the stomach.
Grading	By gradual degrees. Grading of movement means that it can be slow and controlled.
Half kneeling	An upright kneeling position where weight is taken on one knee while the other leg is bent forward with the foot flat on the floor.
Handling	The way in which we move or touch a child.
Hemiplegia	Kind of CP where the whole of one side of a person is affected. It can be either the right or the left side.
Hyper-	Too much.
Hypertonia	Increased tone in muscles. Neural hypertonia is caused by damage to the central nervous system. Non-neural hypertonia is caused by local changes in muscles and joints. If hypertonus is constant, though changing in degree, the child is said to have spasticity.
Hypo-	Too little.
Hypotonia	Low muscle tone.
Inhibition	The ability to suppress one activity in favour of another.
Inversion	Refers to the foot. The foot is inverted when the sole is lifted from the ground and turned inwards to face the other foot while the person is standing.
Inward rotation	The turning inwards of the whole arm or the whole leg. This movement can only take place at the hip or shoulder joint.

Key points of control	Parts of the body from where tone, postures and patterns of movement in other parts can be changed, controlled and guided.
Lateral	Refers to the outer part of a limb or that further away from midline.
Long sitting	Sitting on the floor with legs extended.
Medial	Refers to the inside part of a limb or that closest to midline.
Mobile weight bearing	Bearing weight on limbs or trunk while there is movement, either in the part which is bearing weight or in the rest of the body.
Outward rotation	The turning outwards of the whole arm or the whole leg. This movement can only take place in the hip or shoulder joint.
Over shooting	Inaccurate targeting of a movement such as pointing to or reaching for an object.
Patterns of movement	When normal patterns of movement take place in a huge variety of ways to carry out everyday activities such as walking. *Abnormal patterns* are seen in a child with spasticity who can only move in a few stereotyped ways that are not functionally useful.
Pelvis	Bony framework that includes the pelvic bones and hip joints.
Plantarflexion	Movement at the ankle joint when the toes are down and the heel up; standing on the toes.
Postural control	Ability to hold the body steady before, during and after a movement.
Posture	The position in which a person holds himself or herself.
Posterior	Behind or at the back.
Prone	Lying on the flexor surface of the body. The face can be down or turned to the side.
Protective reactions	Automatic movements that act to protect the body from injury, e.g., stretching out arms to protect face or taking a step to avoid falling.
Proximal-Proximally	Close to central parts of the body.
Pull to stand	Before a young child can stand up from the floor alone, he pulls himself up by holding on to the furniture or his mother. This is called pulling to stand.
Reciprocal movement	Complementary opposite movements as one leg moving forward and the other backwards during walking.
Righting reaction	Automatic responses that work with equilibrium reactions to bring head and trunk back into alignment after activity.

Rotation	Movement of one part of the body round the body axis. For example, a person rotates the trunk when he twists the top half of the body to one side, leaving the lower part of the body in a neutral position.
Sacrum	Saddle shaped bone at the base of the spine that joins the two halves of the pelvis together.
Shoulder girdle	The bony framework that includes the collar bone and the shoulder blade.
Side lying	Lying on either the right or the left side.
Spasticity-Spastic	Abnormal stiffness in muscles that makes a child move in a limited stereotyped way or may even make movement impossible.
Sternum	The breast bone.
Supine	Lying on the extensor surface of the body. The face may be up or turned to either side.
Symmetry	Both sides of the body are the same.
Tendo-Achilles	Muscle tendon attaching calf muscle to heel bone. It is sometimes called the heel cord.
Tone	State of tension in muscles, or state of readiness to become tense or move.
Windswept	A child's legs are described as windswept when one leg is more in abduction, flexion and outward rotation and the other more in adduction, extension and inward rotation. The legs look as if they have been blown to one side.

Index

About the Author

Archie Hinchcliffe, who is based in Hutton in the UK, is a consultant Physiotherapy Trainer specialising in training therapist and community workers working with children in developing countries. She has had extensive hands-on experience working with children with cerebral palsy, as well as with therapists and community workers, in a large range of countries including Jordan, Syria, South Africa, Afghanistan, Kuwait, Zambia and Tanzania.